Halloween
MOUNTS 4
Coloring book

AUTHOR AND ILLUSTRATOR
OLGA GOLOVESHKINA

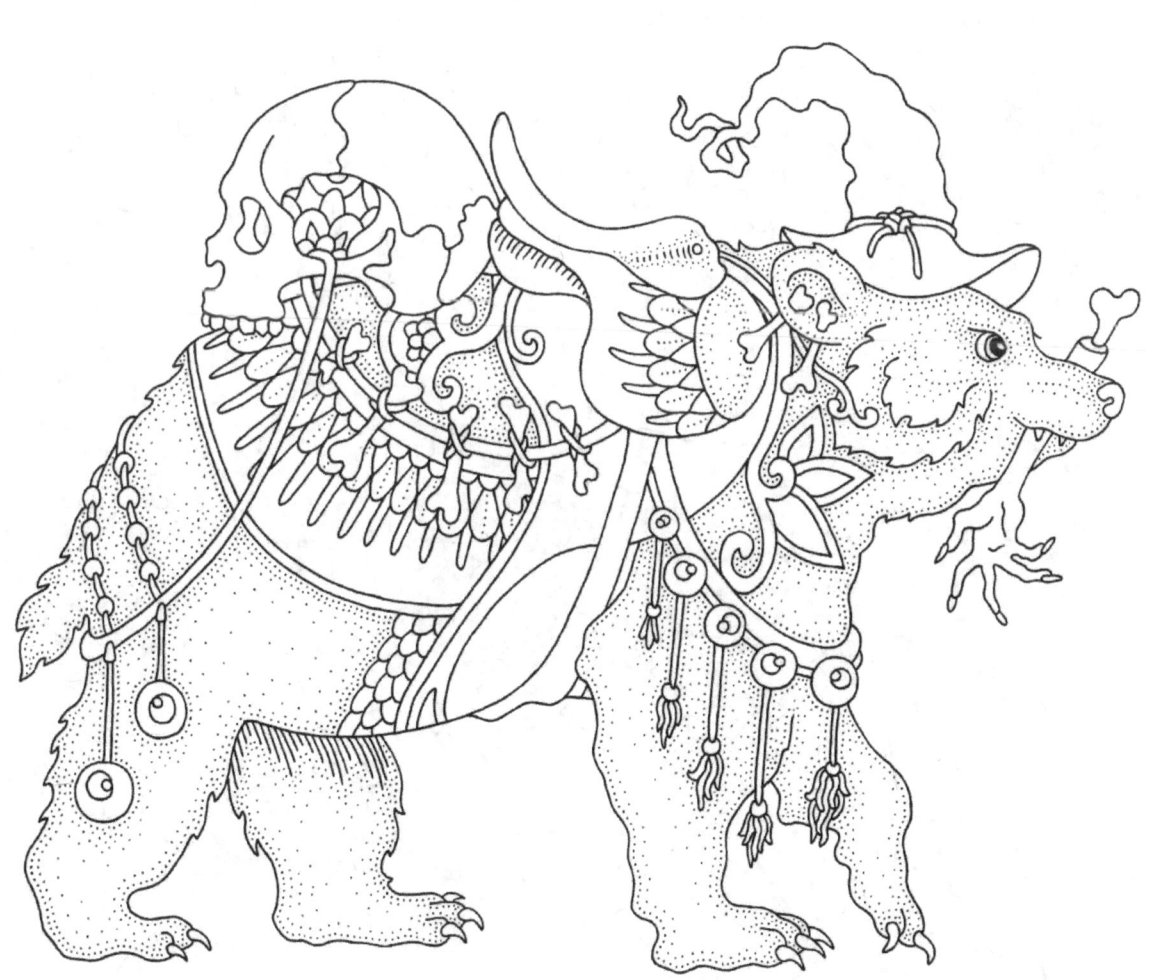

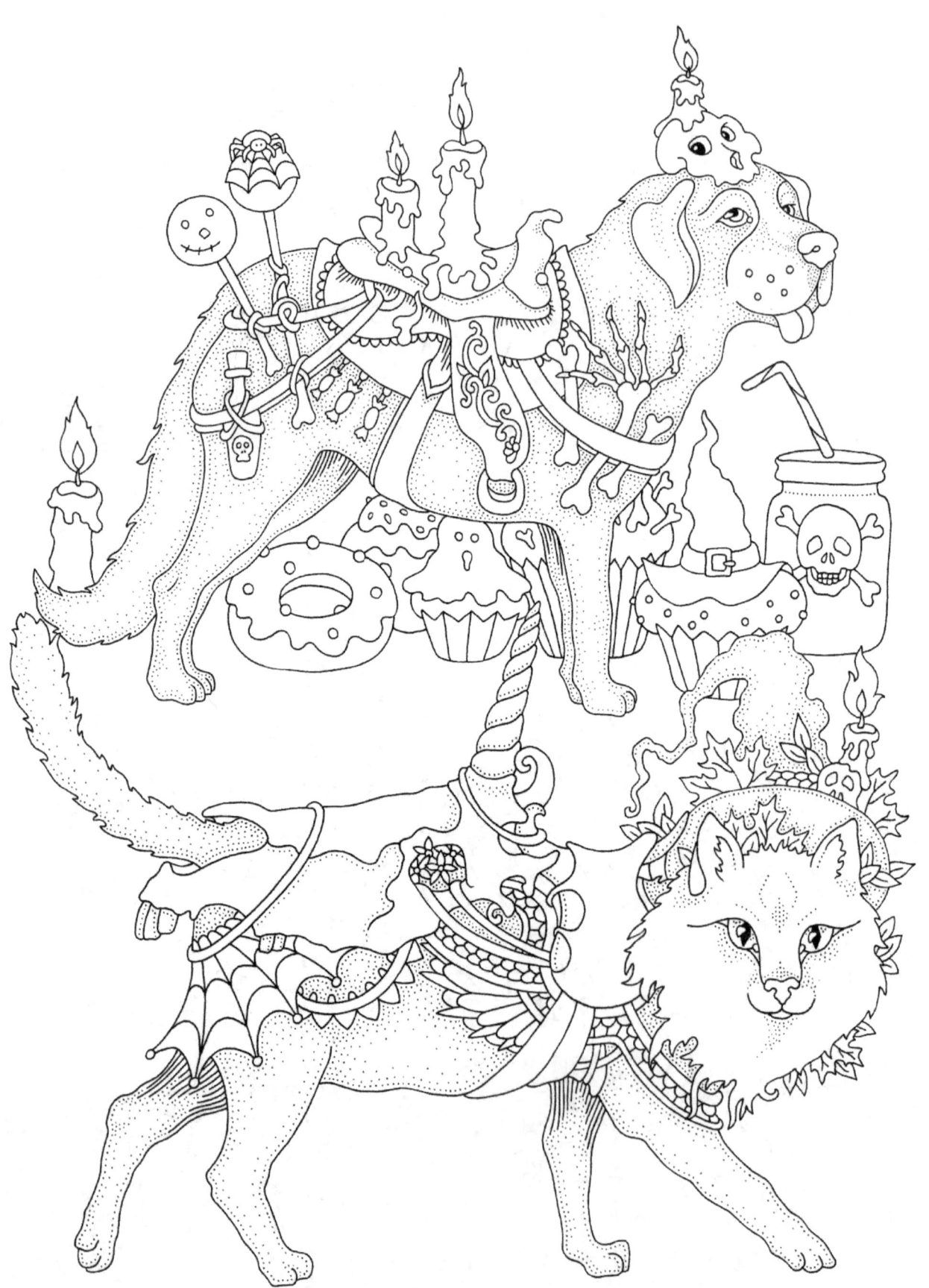

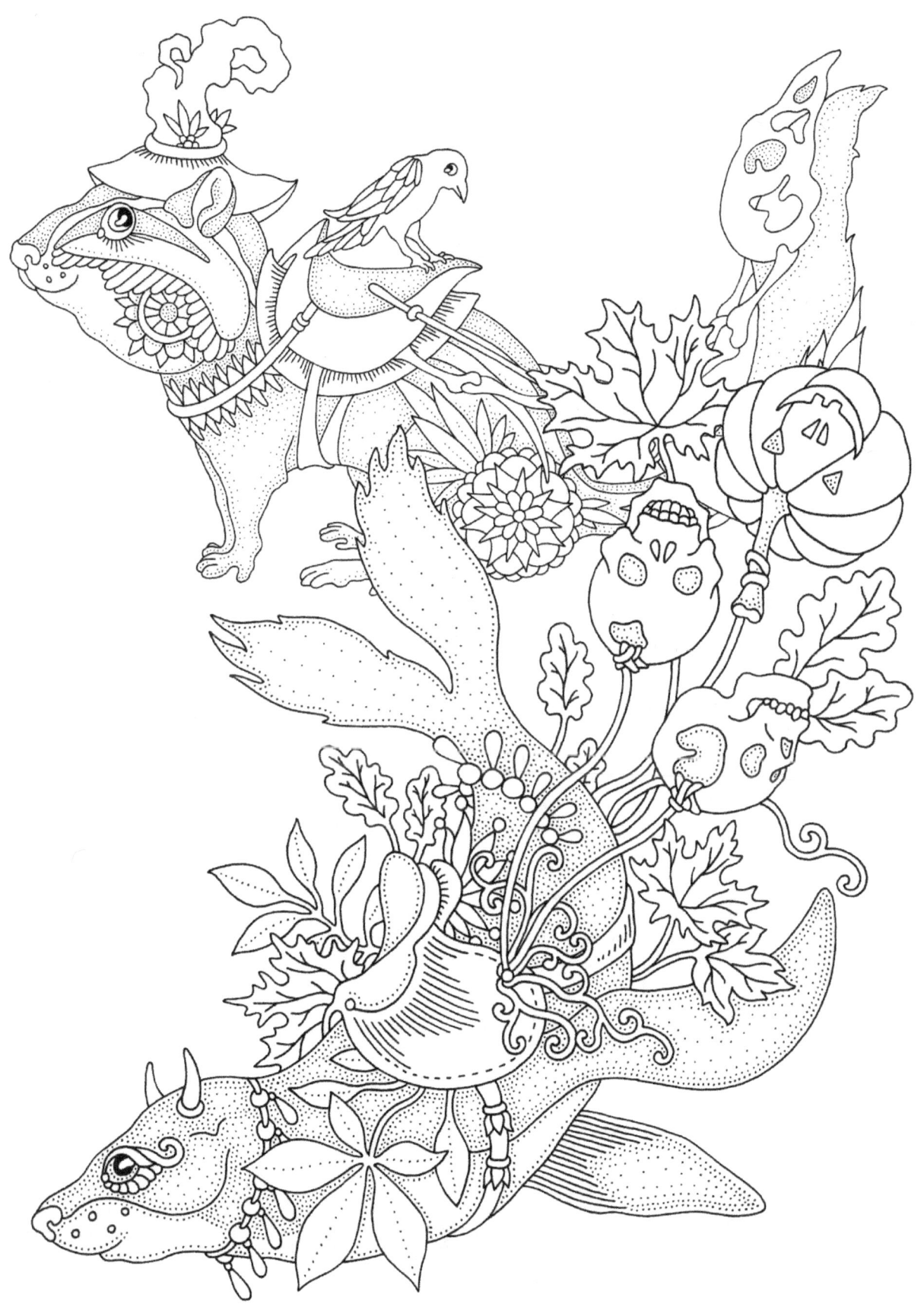

Copyright © 2017 Olga Goloveshkina

All rights reserved.

ISBN 1977797857
ISBN-13:9781977797858

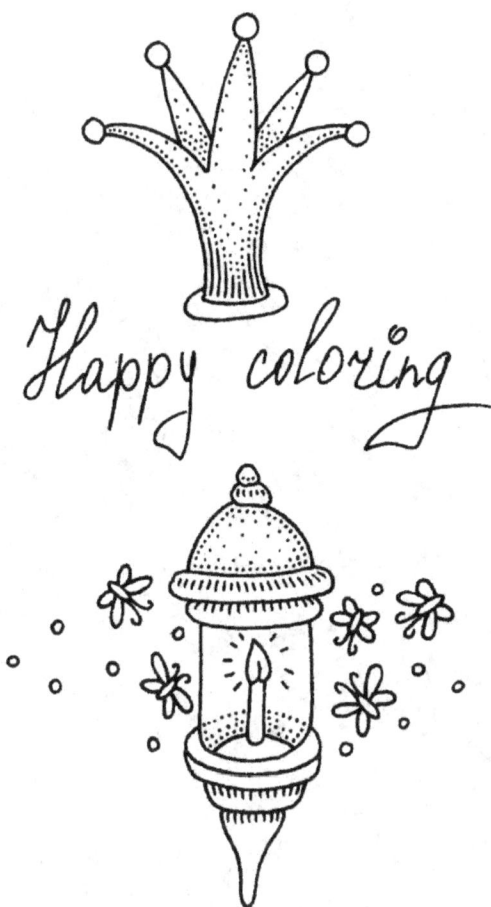

Happy coloring

Thank you for choosing my coloring book!

Olya :)

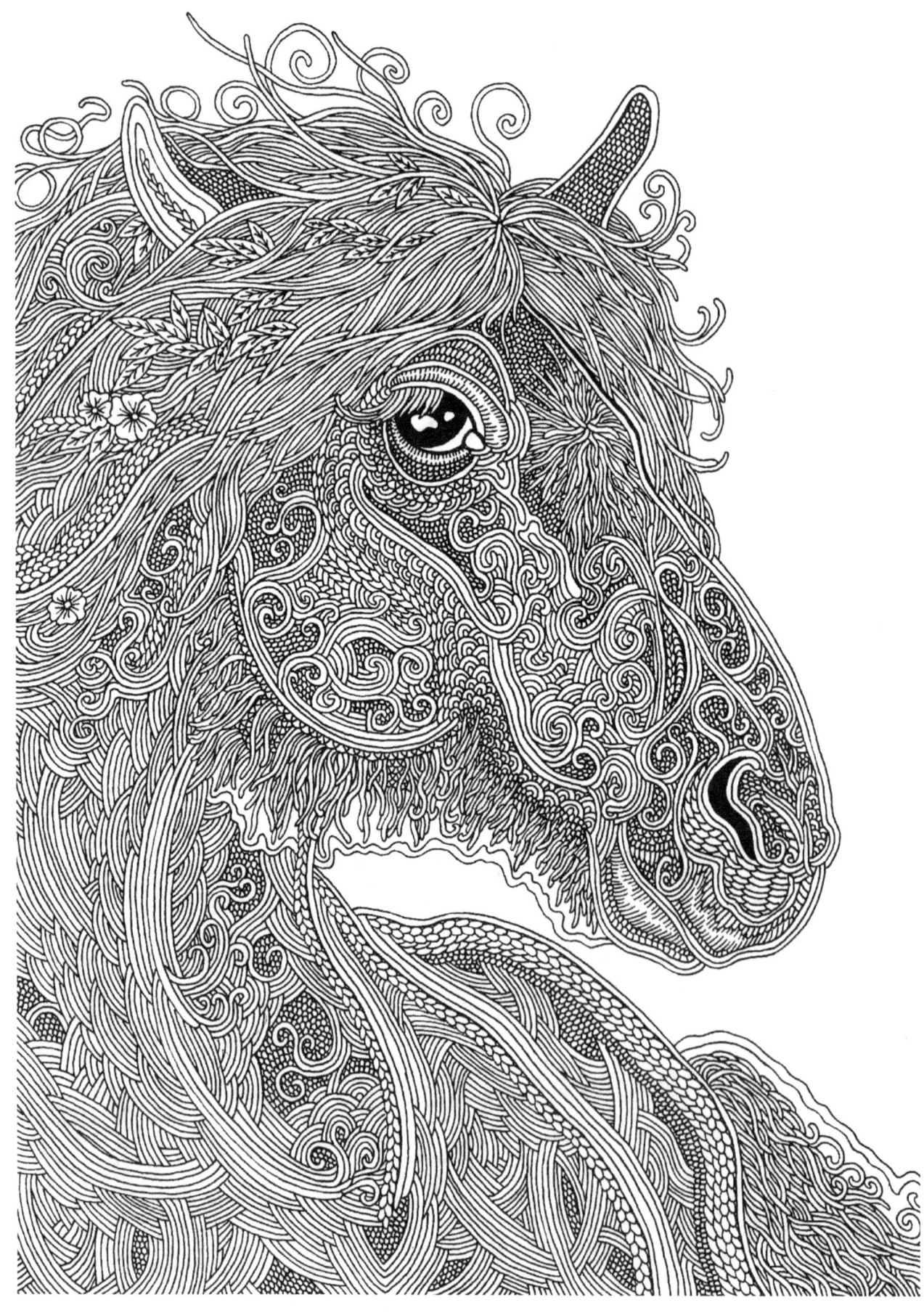

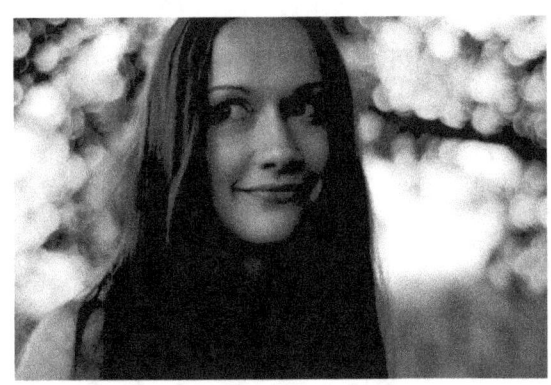

ABOUT THE AUTHOR

Olga Goloveshkina is a freelance artist and illustrator based in Moscow, Russia.
She graduated from the Institute of Business and Design.
Olga specializes in black ink doodles.
She is an author and illustrator coloring books for adults:
1. "The wind carries flowers"/"Veter unosit tsvety" (in Russian, 2015),
2. "Fox travel: Coloring book" (in English, 2016),
3. "Mounts" (in English, 2016),
4. "Mounts 2" (in English, 2016),
5. "Enchanted horses" (in English, 2016),
6. "Horse and Architecture" (in English, 2016),
7. "Alice in Wonderland Coloring Book" (in English, 2017),
8. "Mounts 3" zodiac coloring book (in English, 2017),
9. "Mounts 4" Halloween coloring book (in English, 2017).

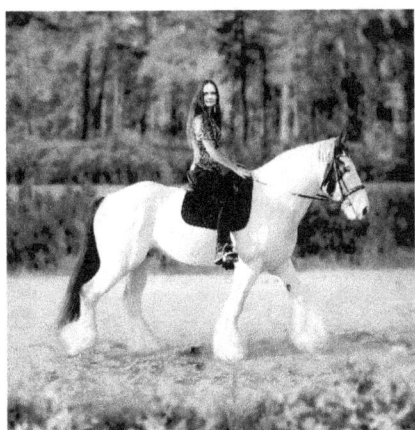

Author page on Amazon:
amazon.com/author/olgagoloveshkina
Site: http://olyagoloveshkina.jimdo.com
etsy.com/shop/OlyaColoringBook
Instagram:
@olyahitrayapanda

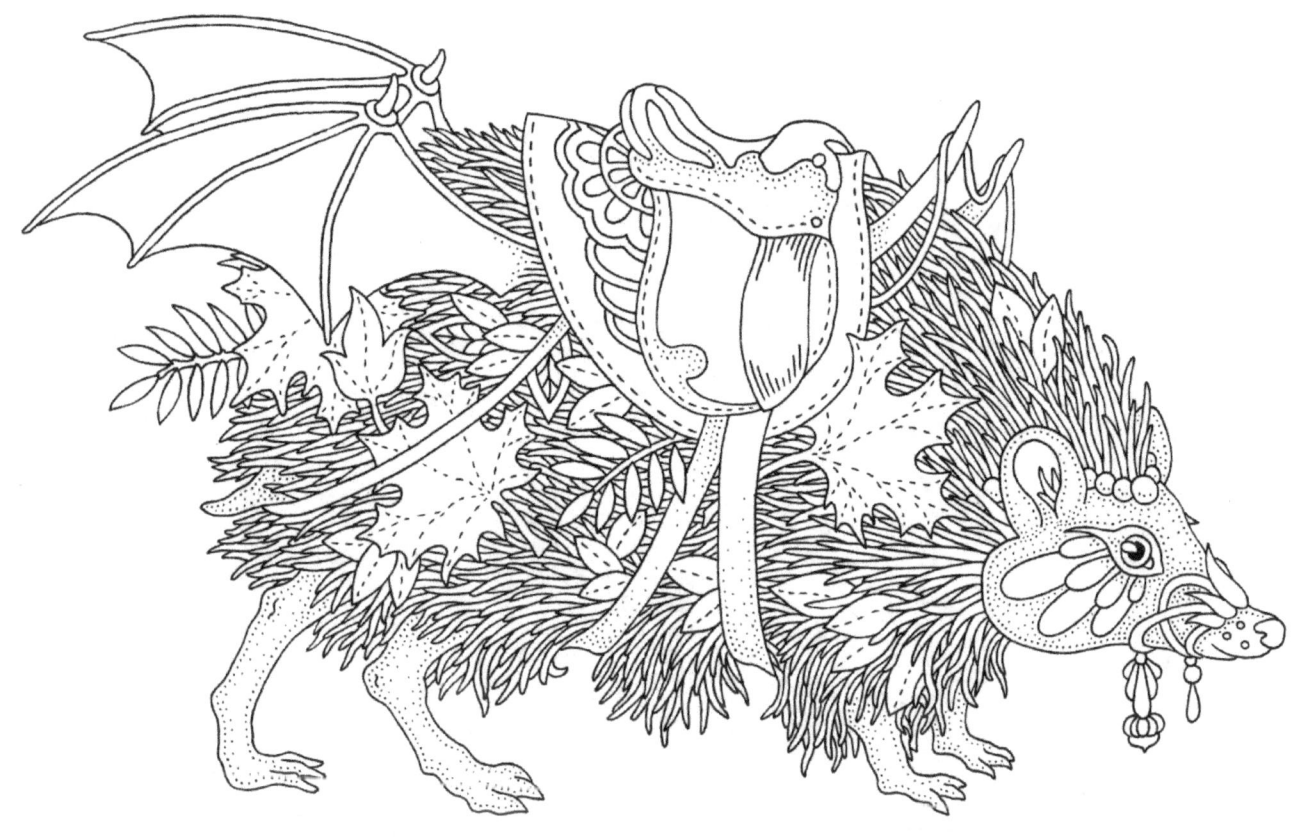

This book belongs to

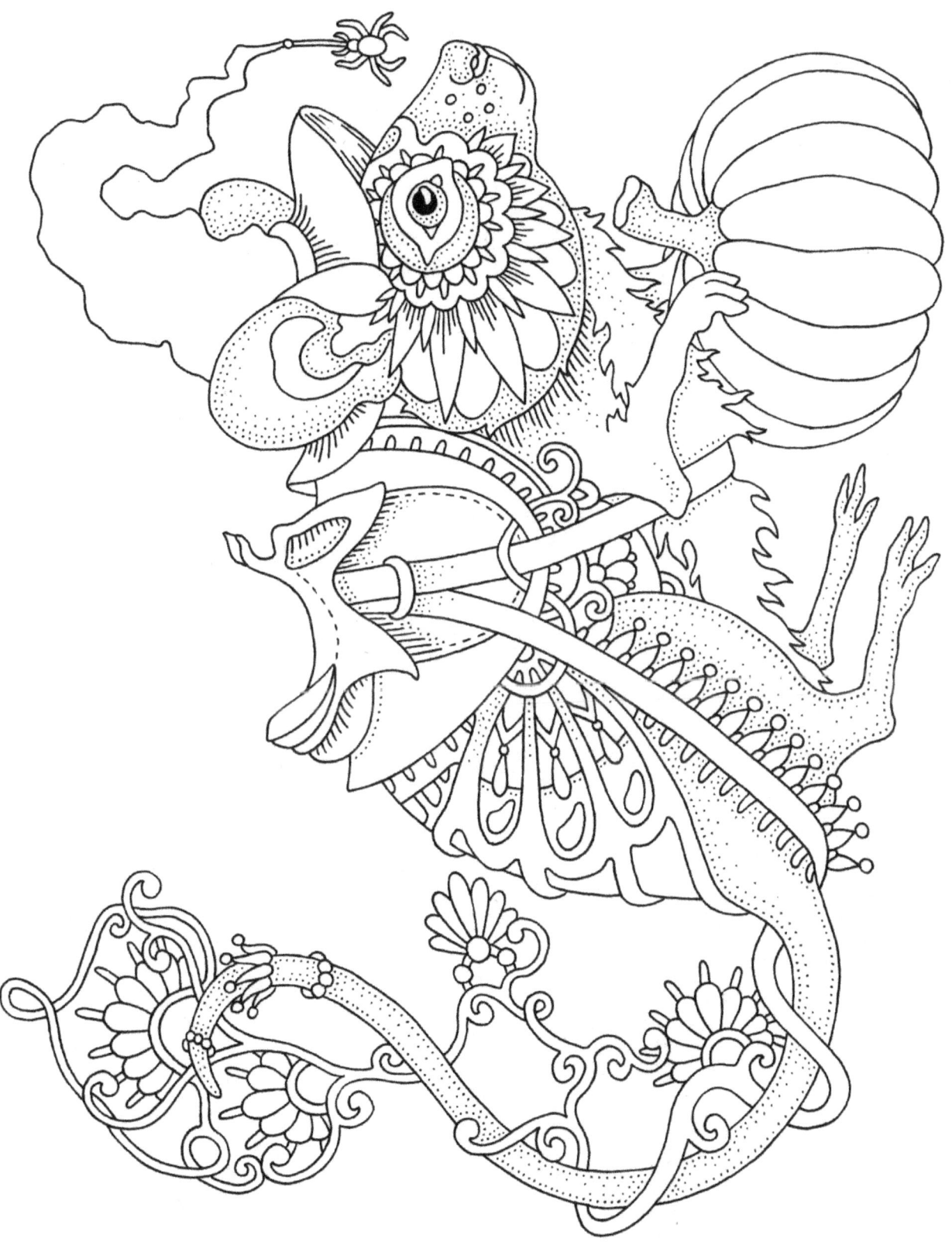

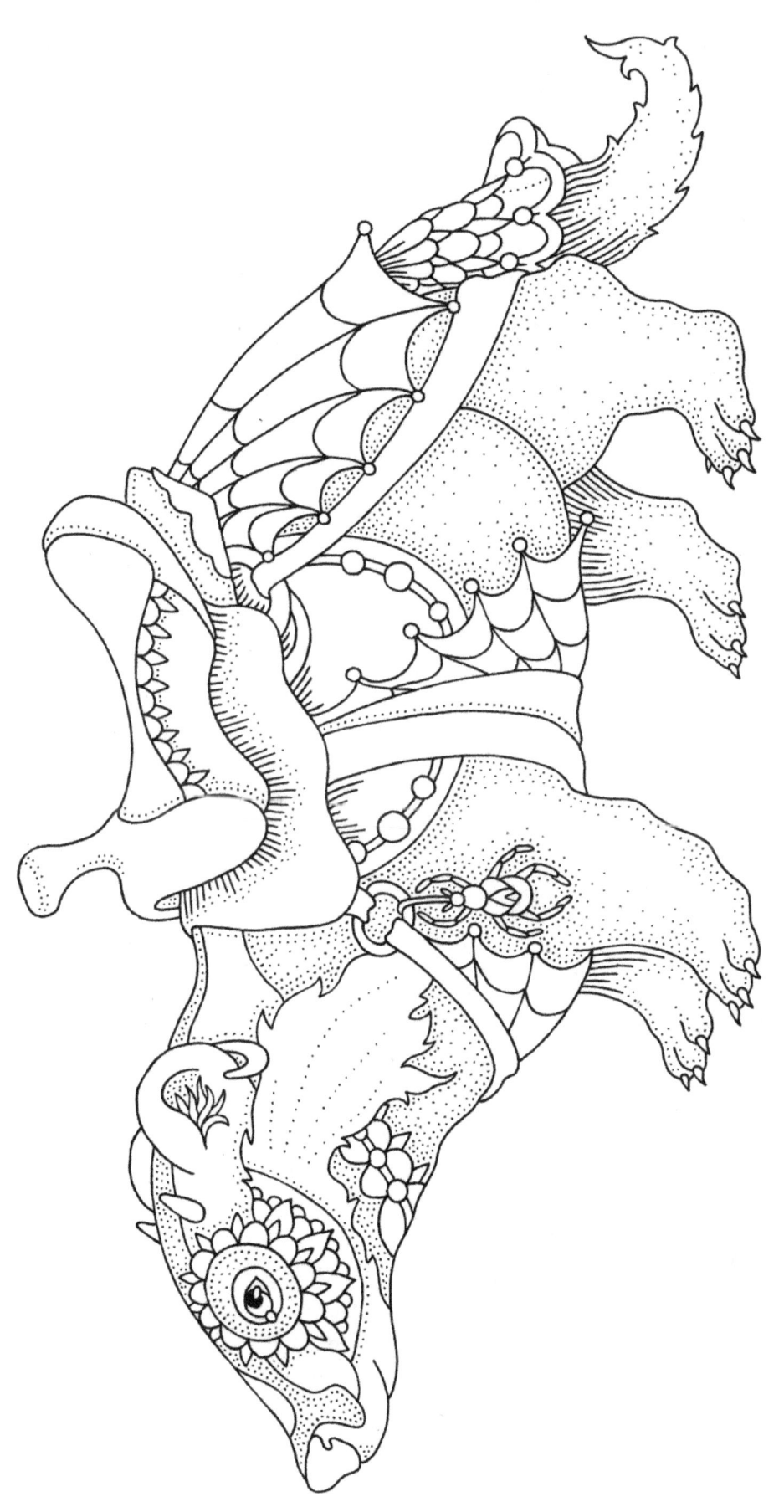

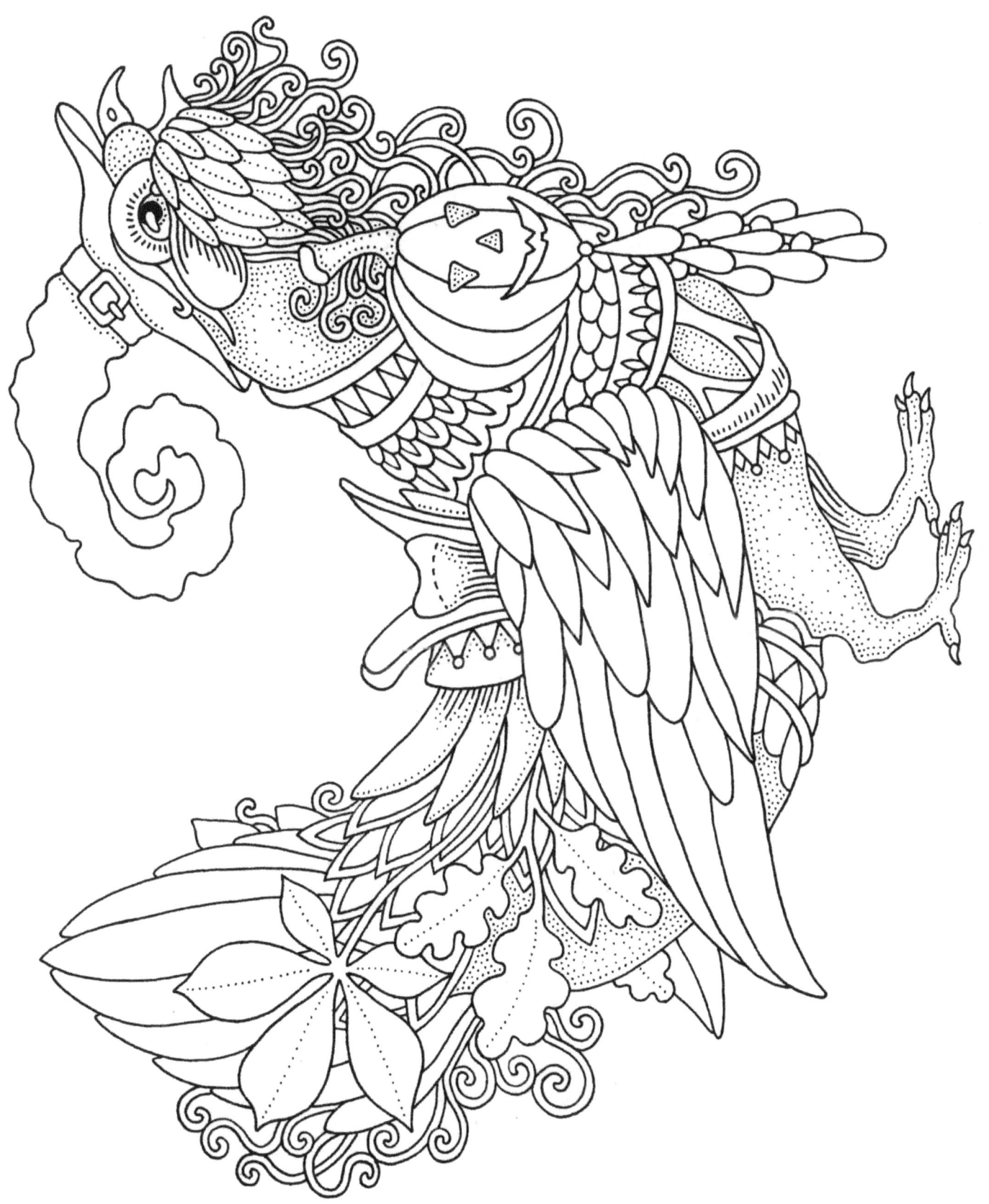

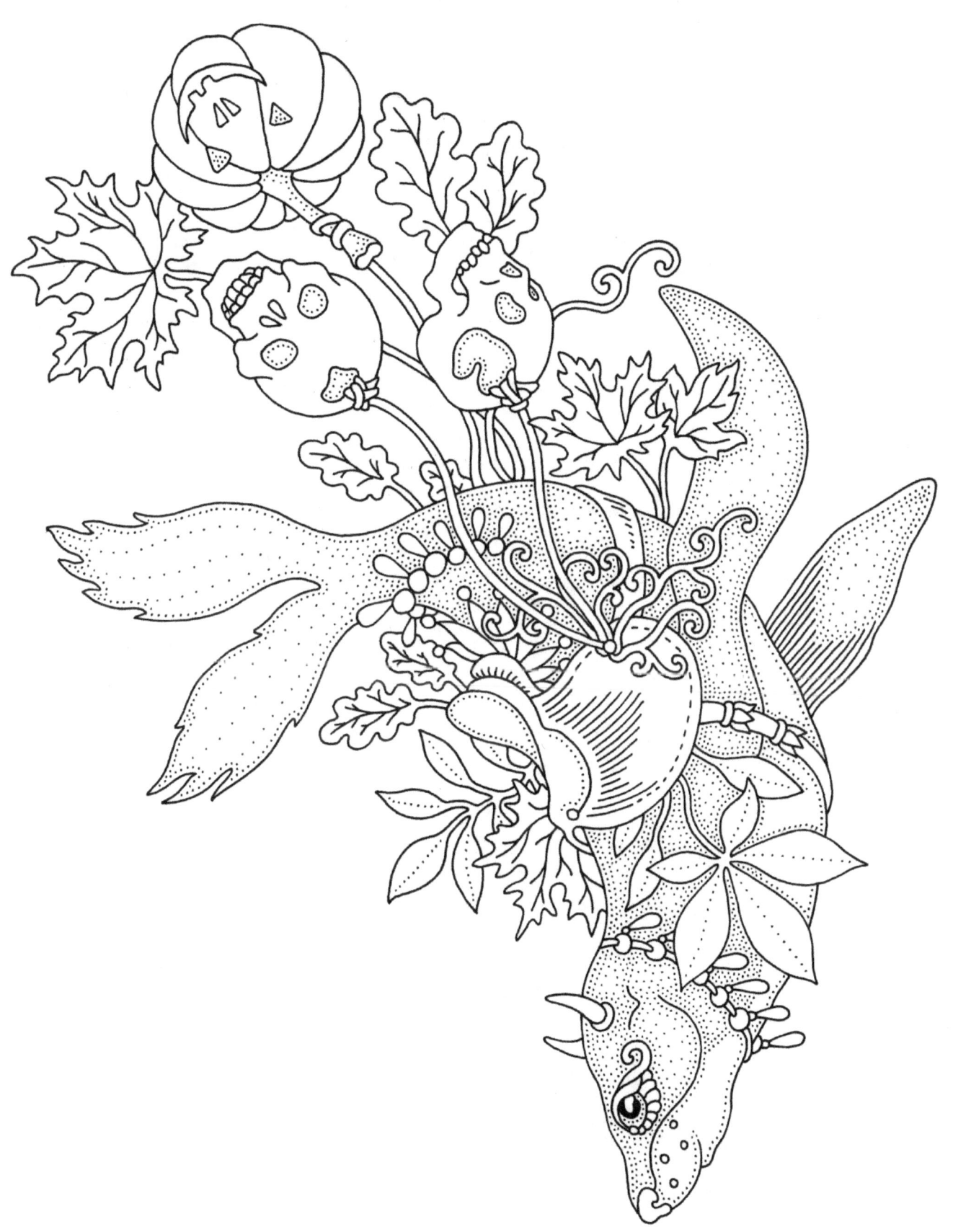

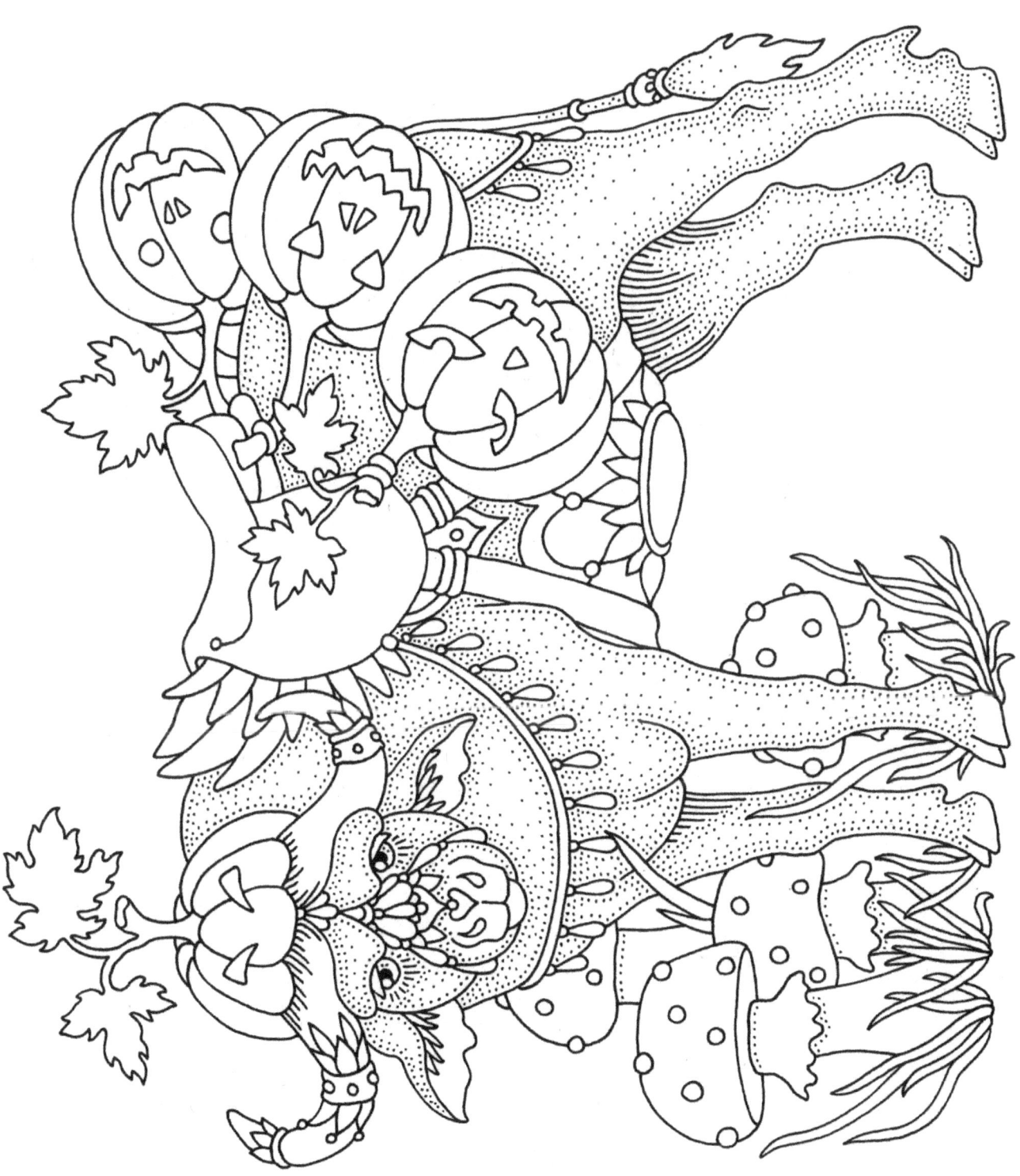

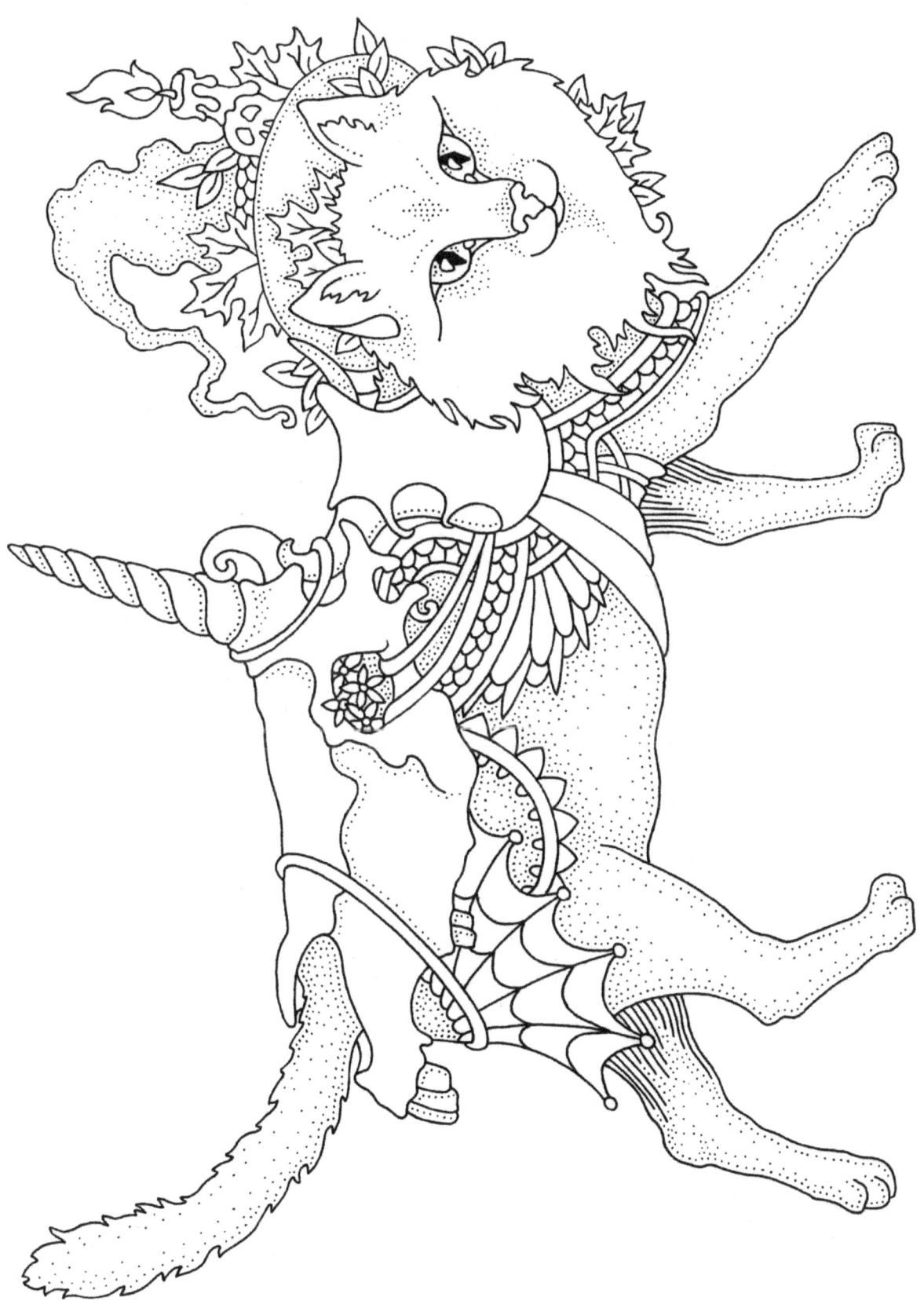

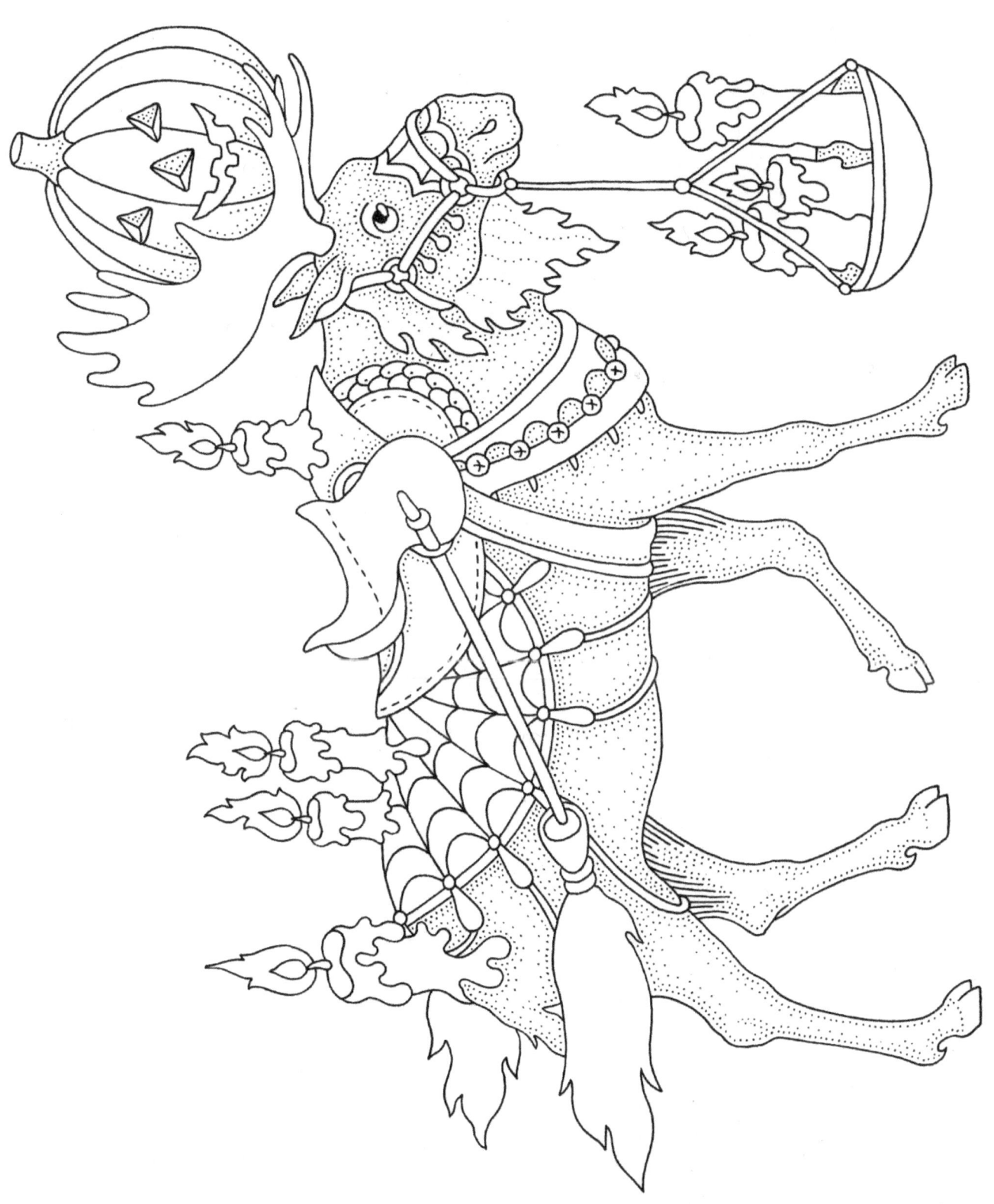

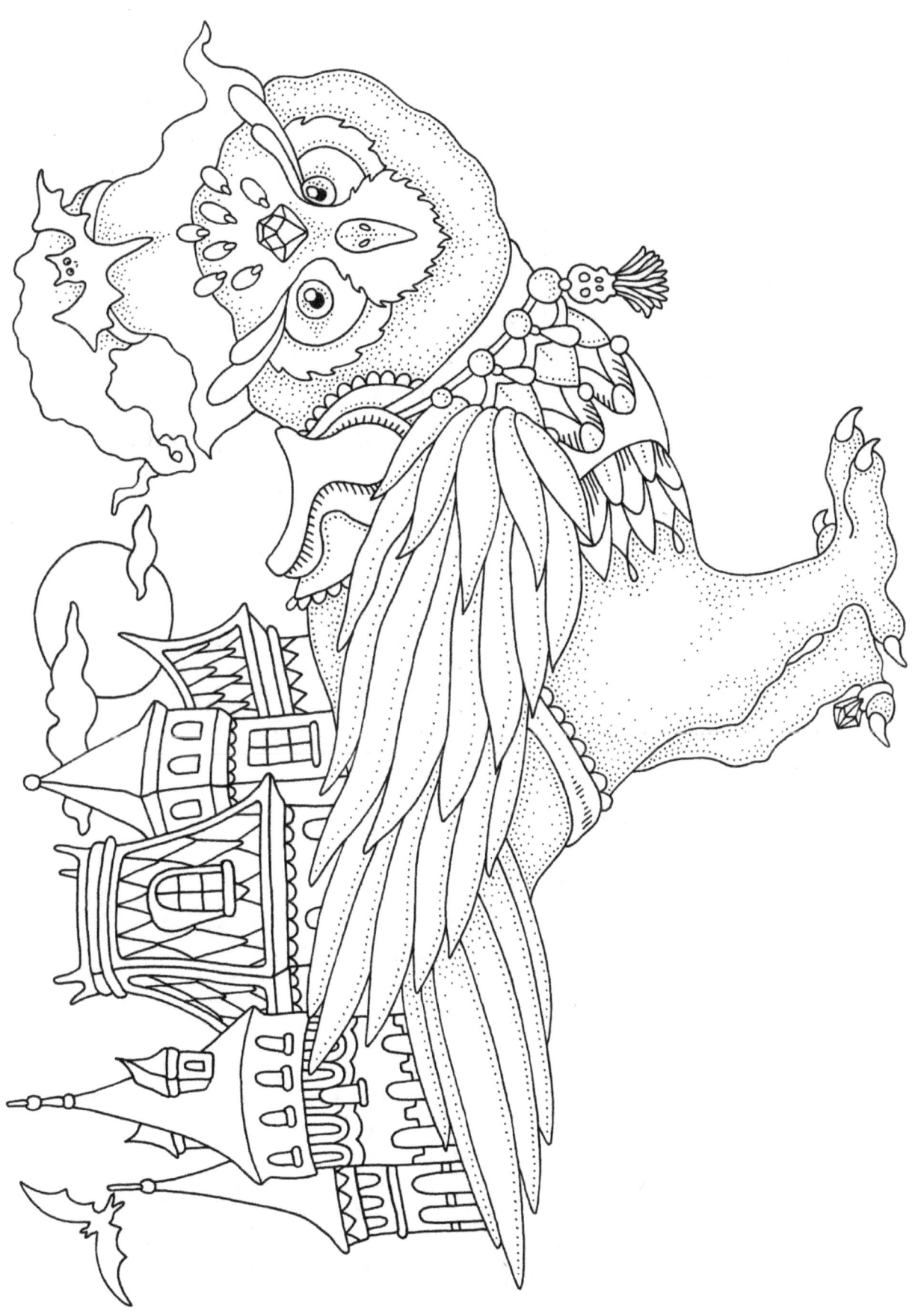

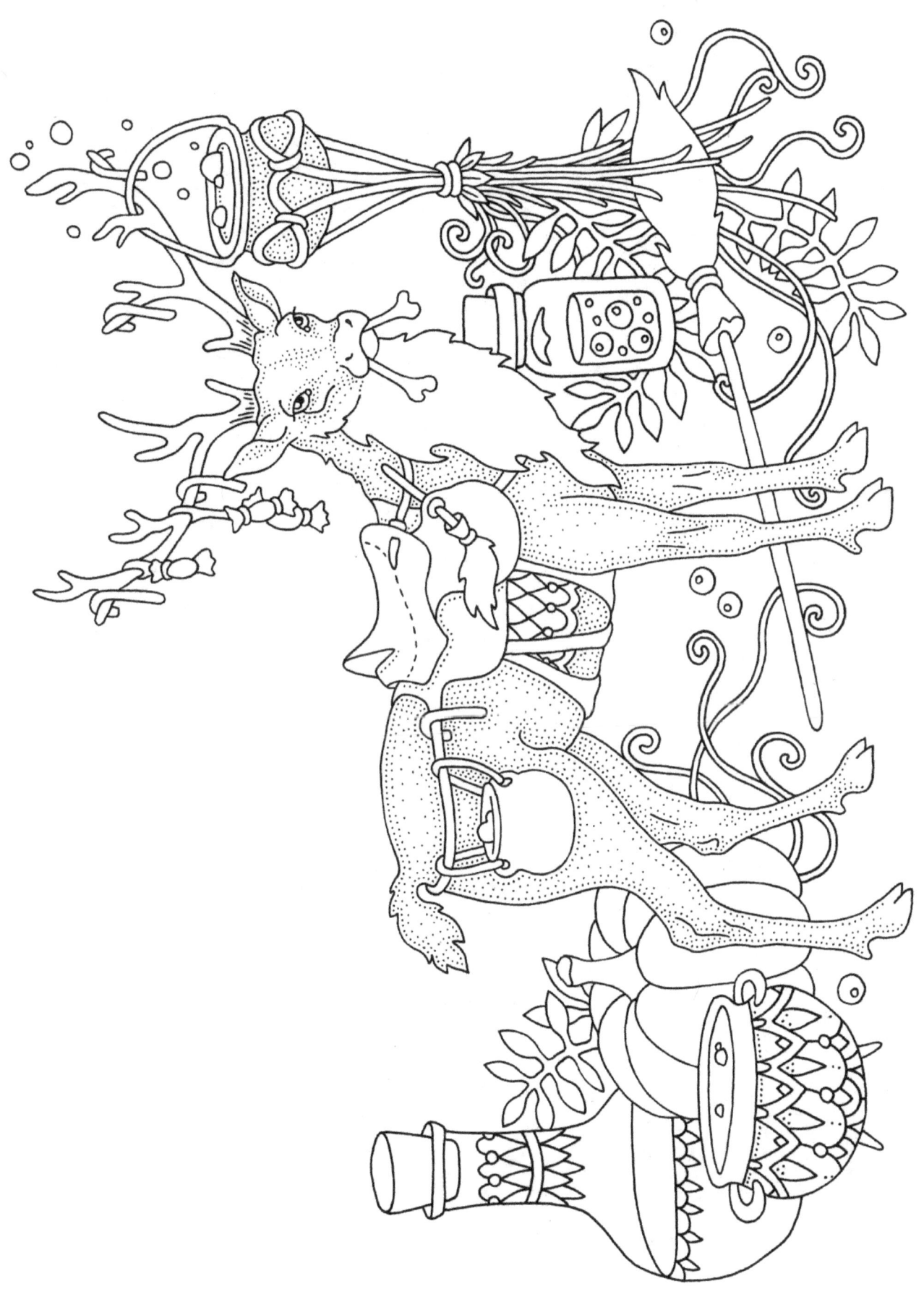

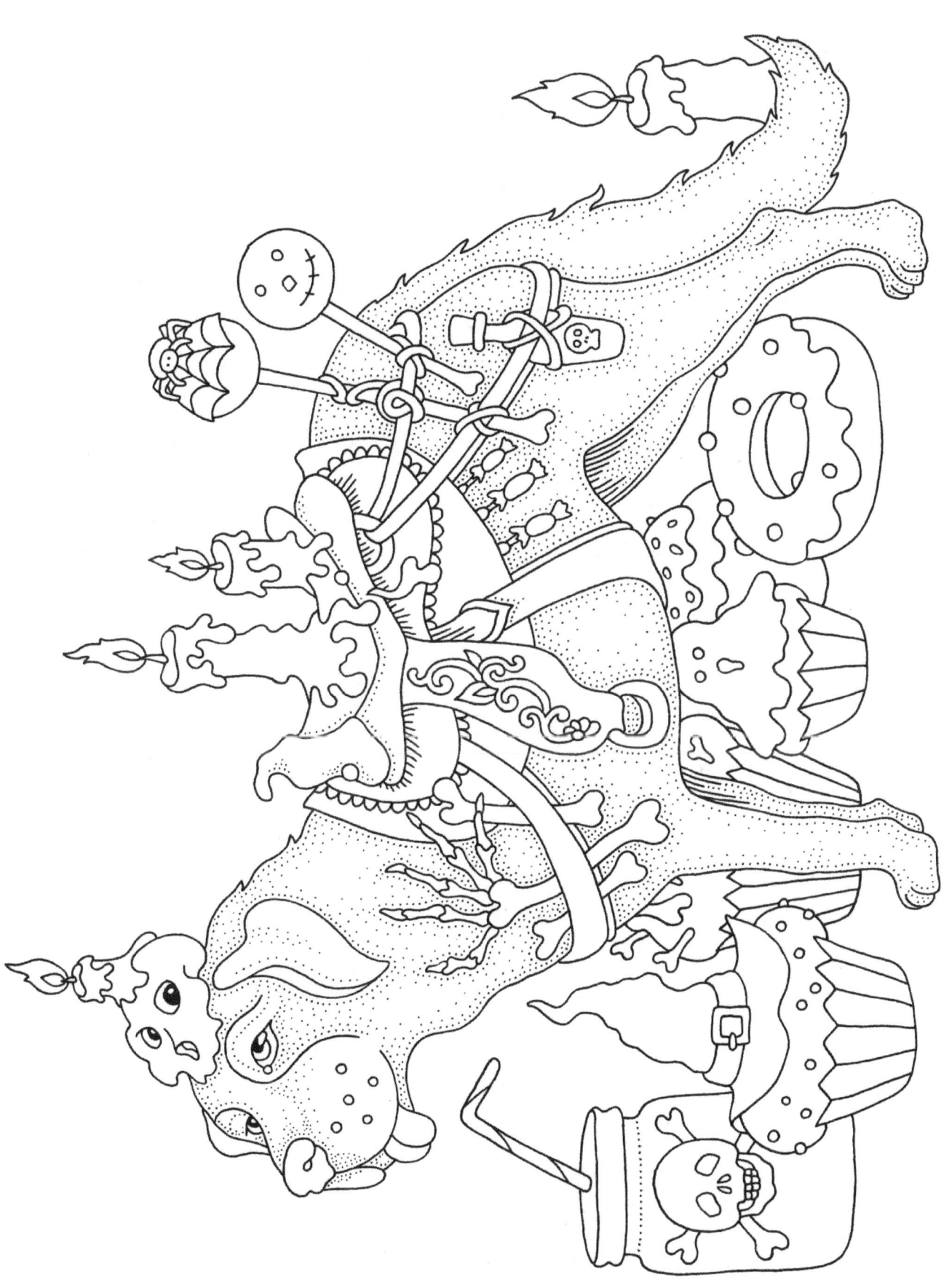

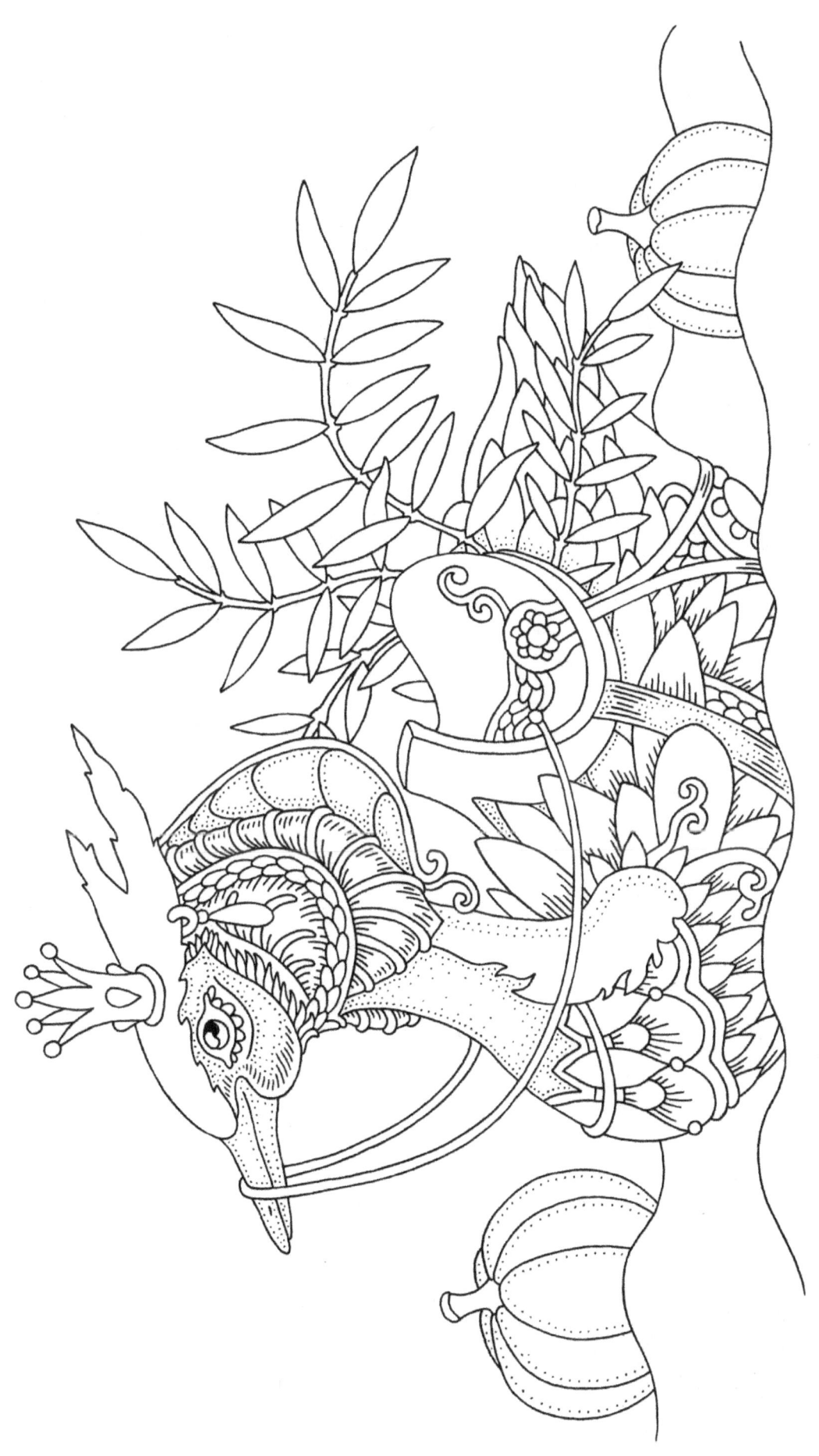

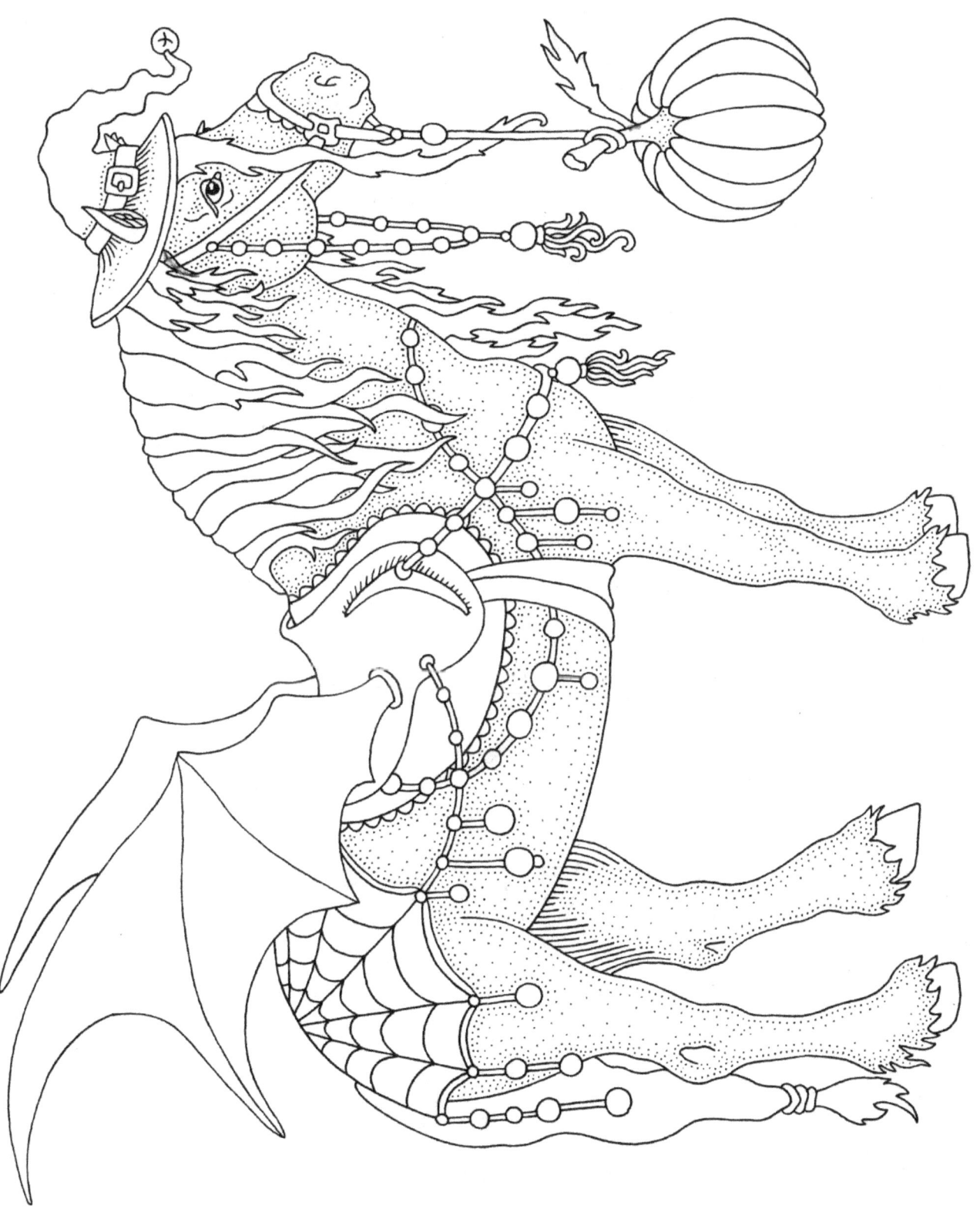

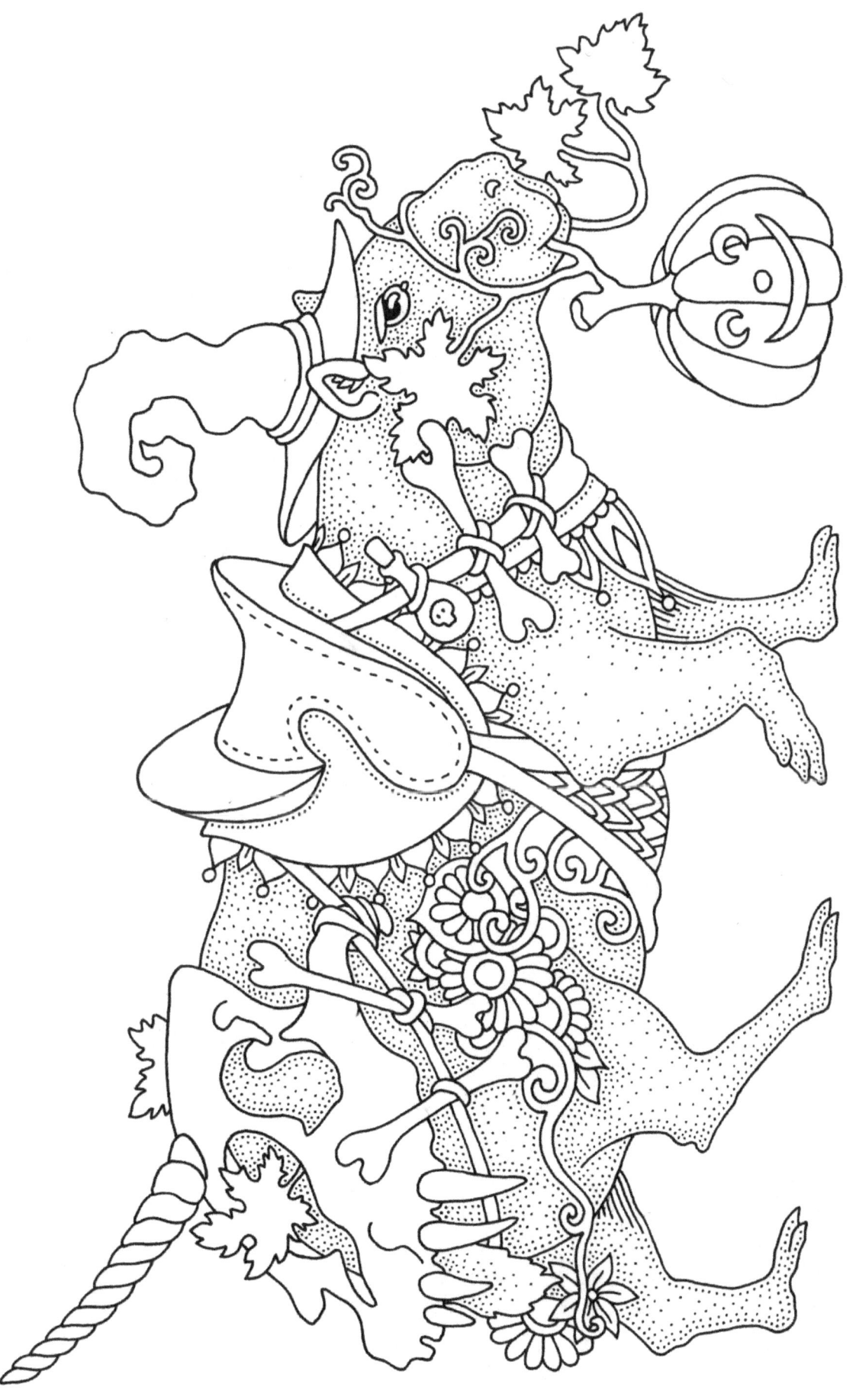

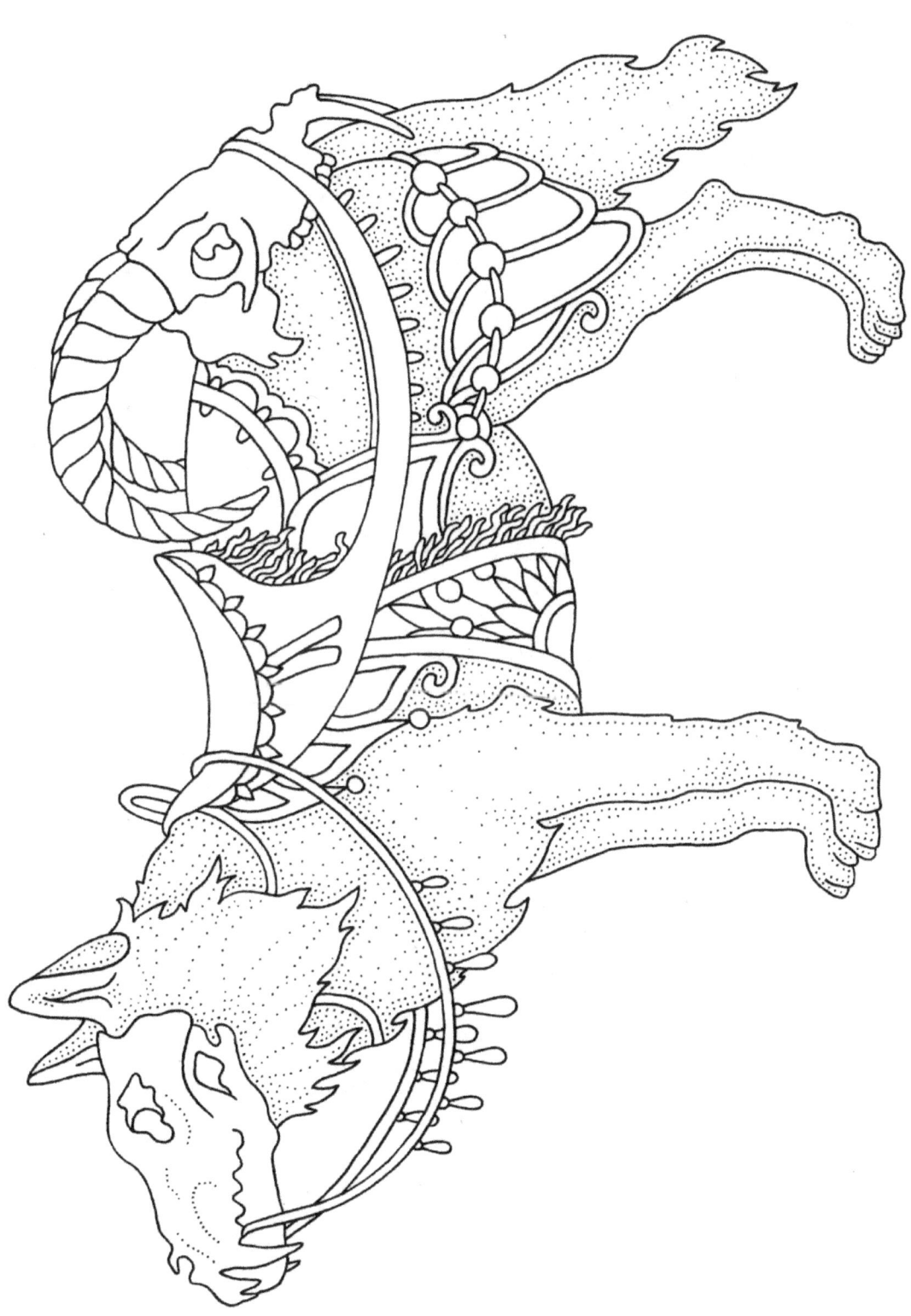

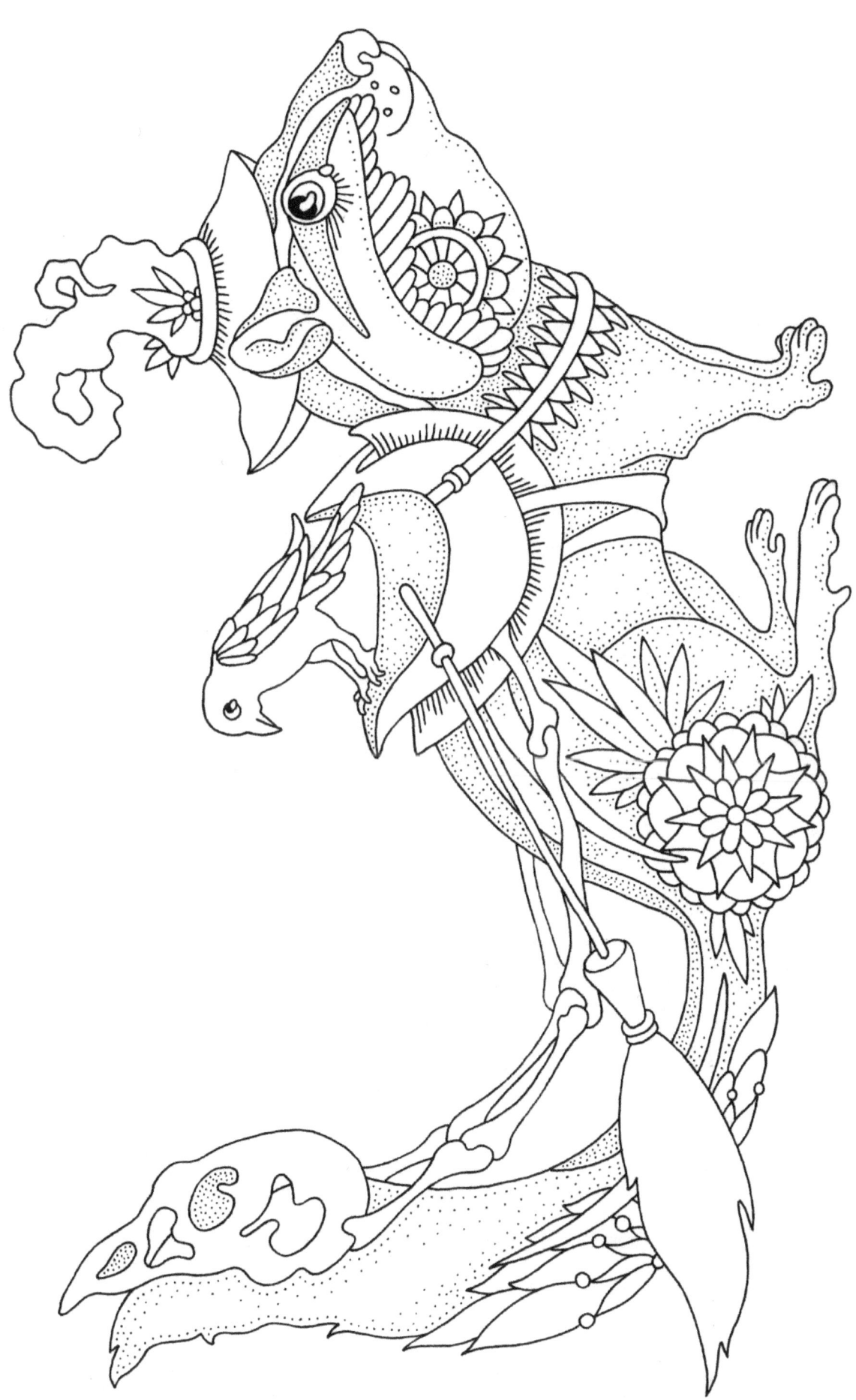

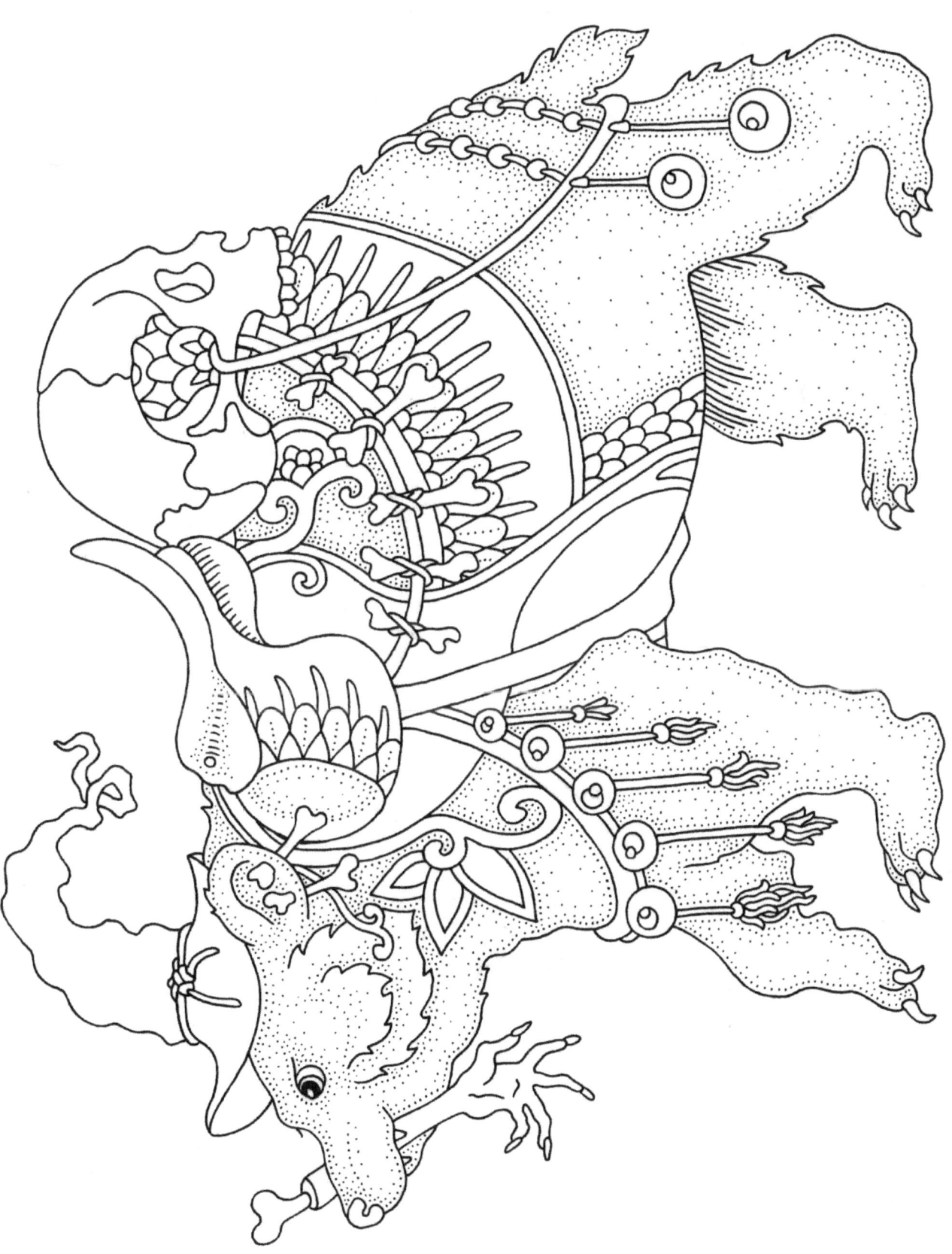

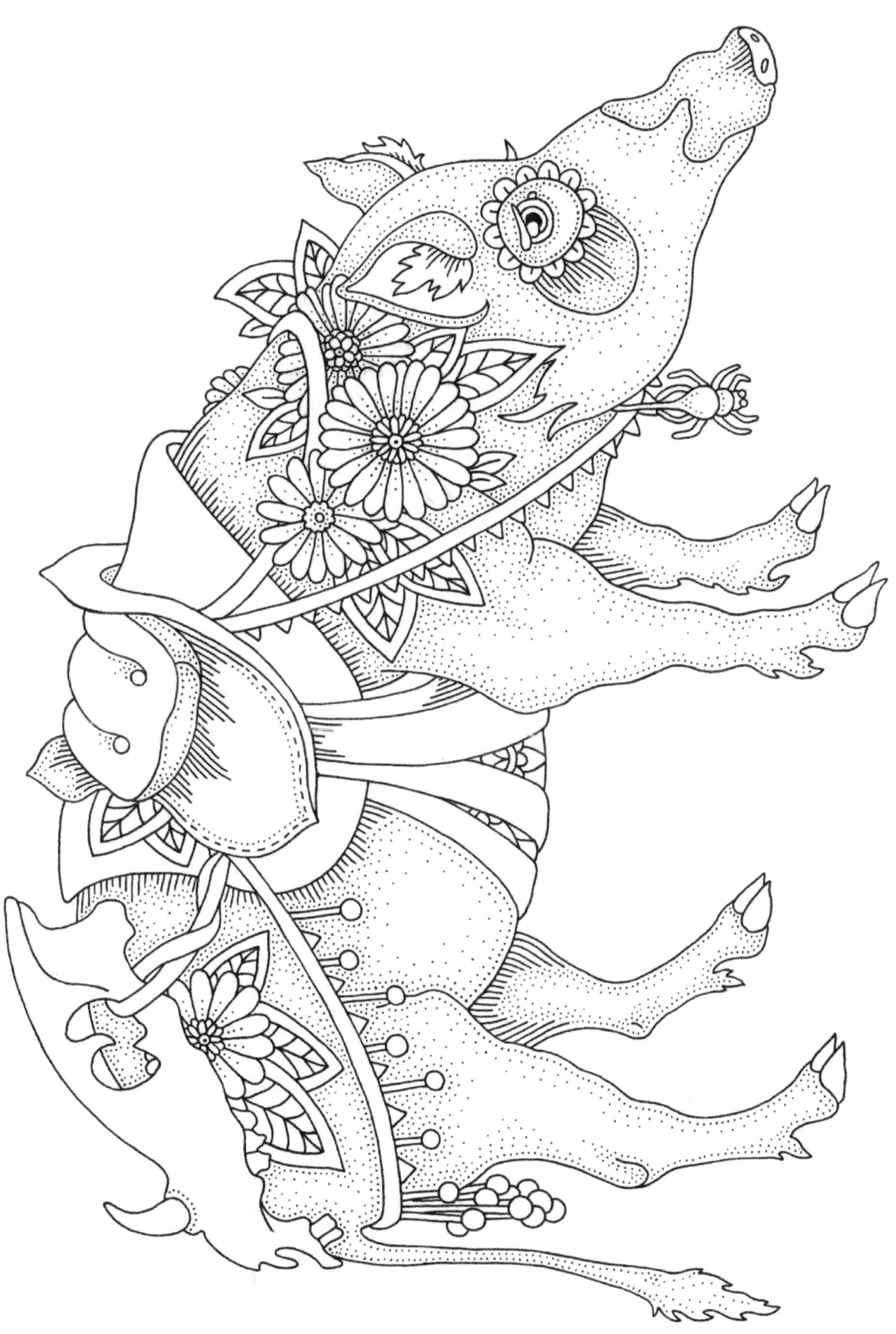

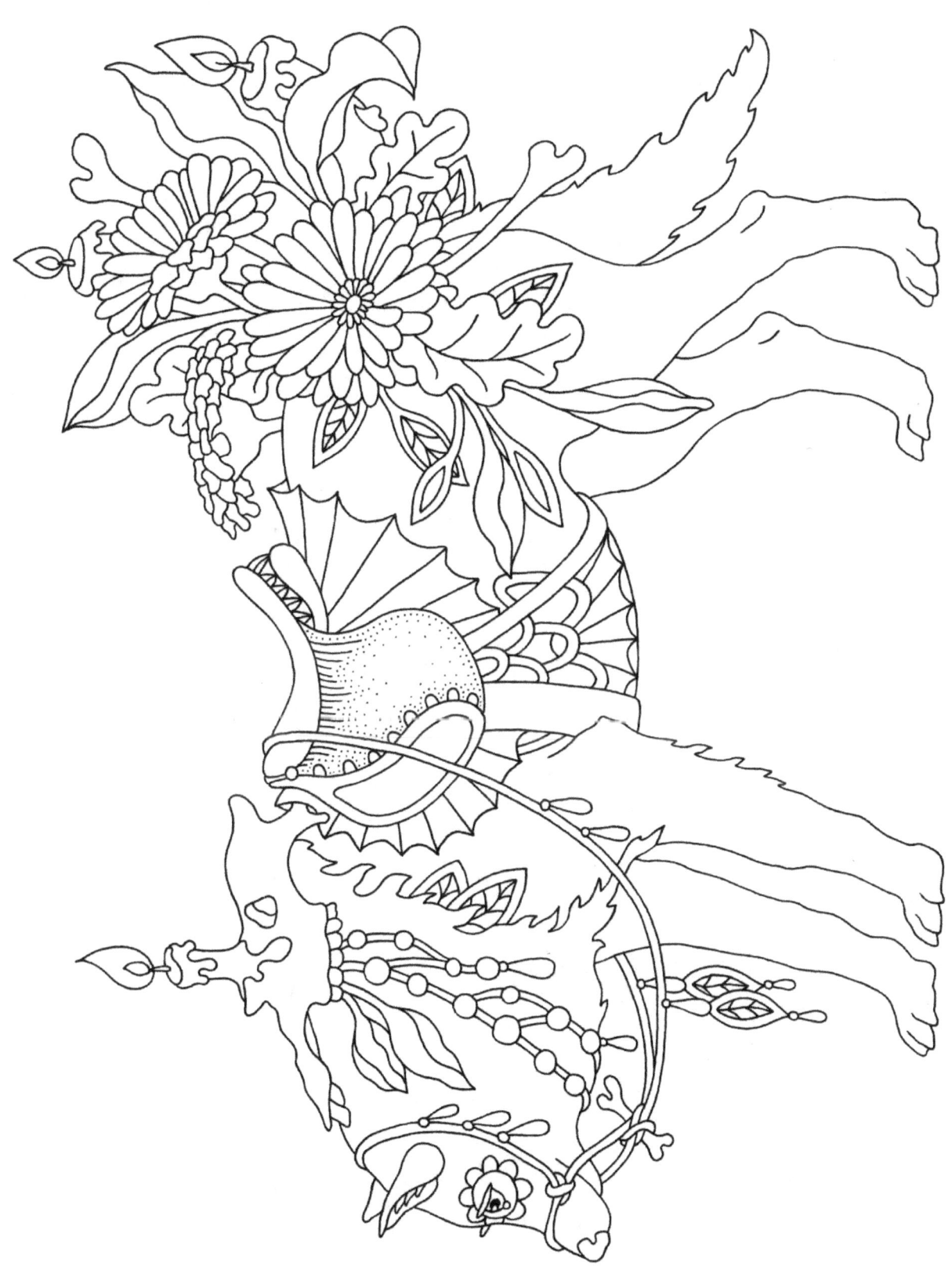

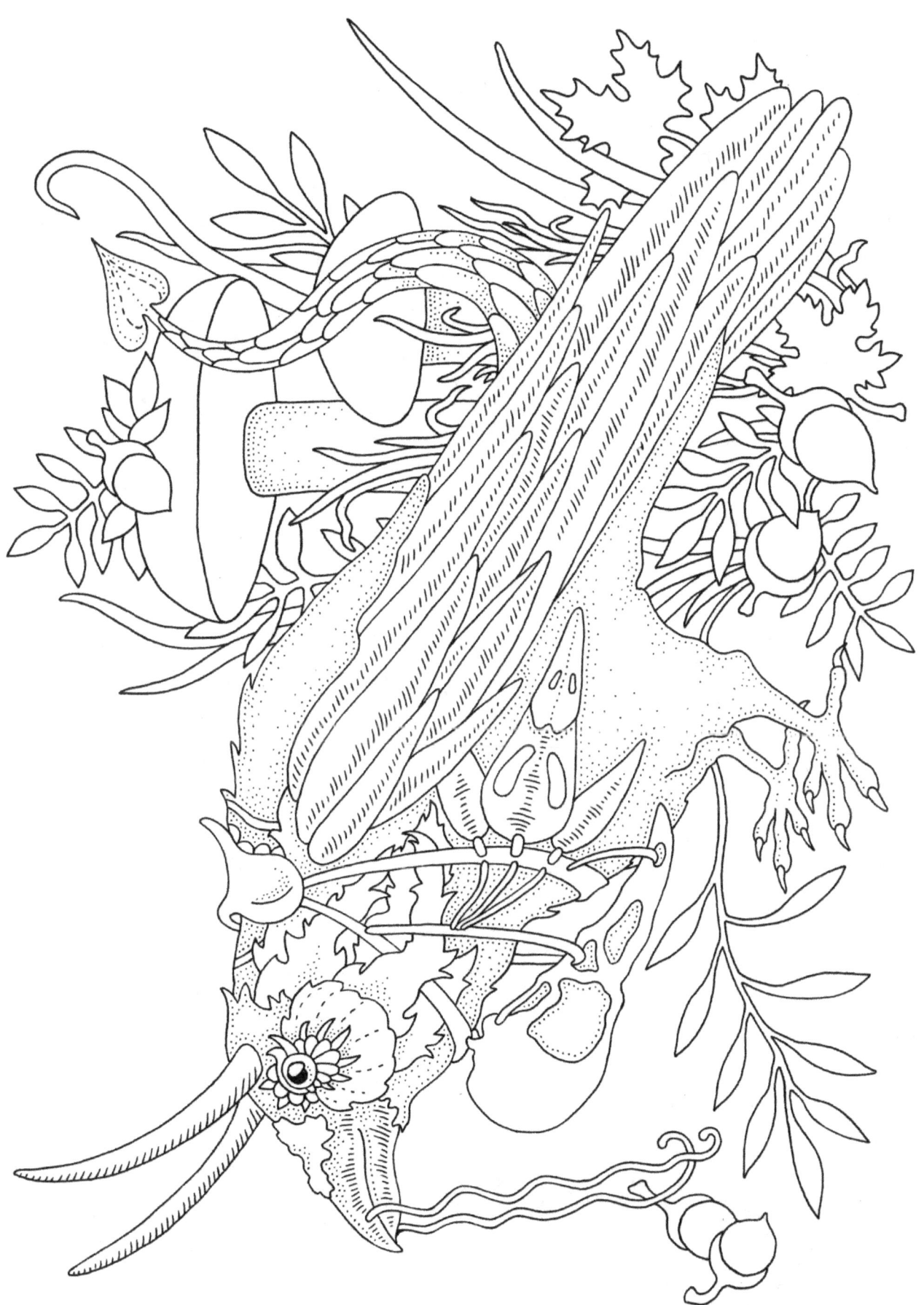

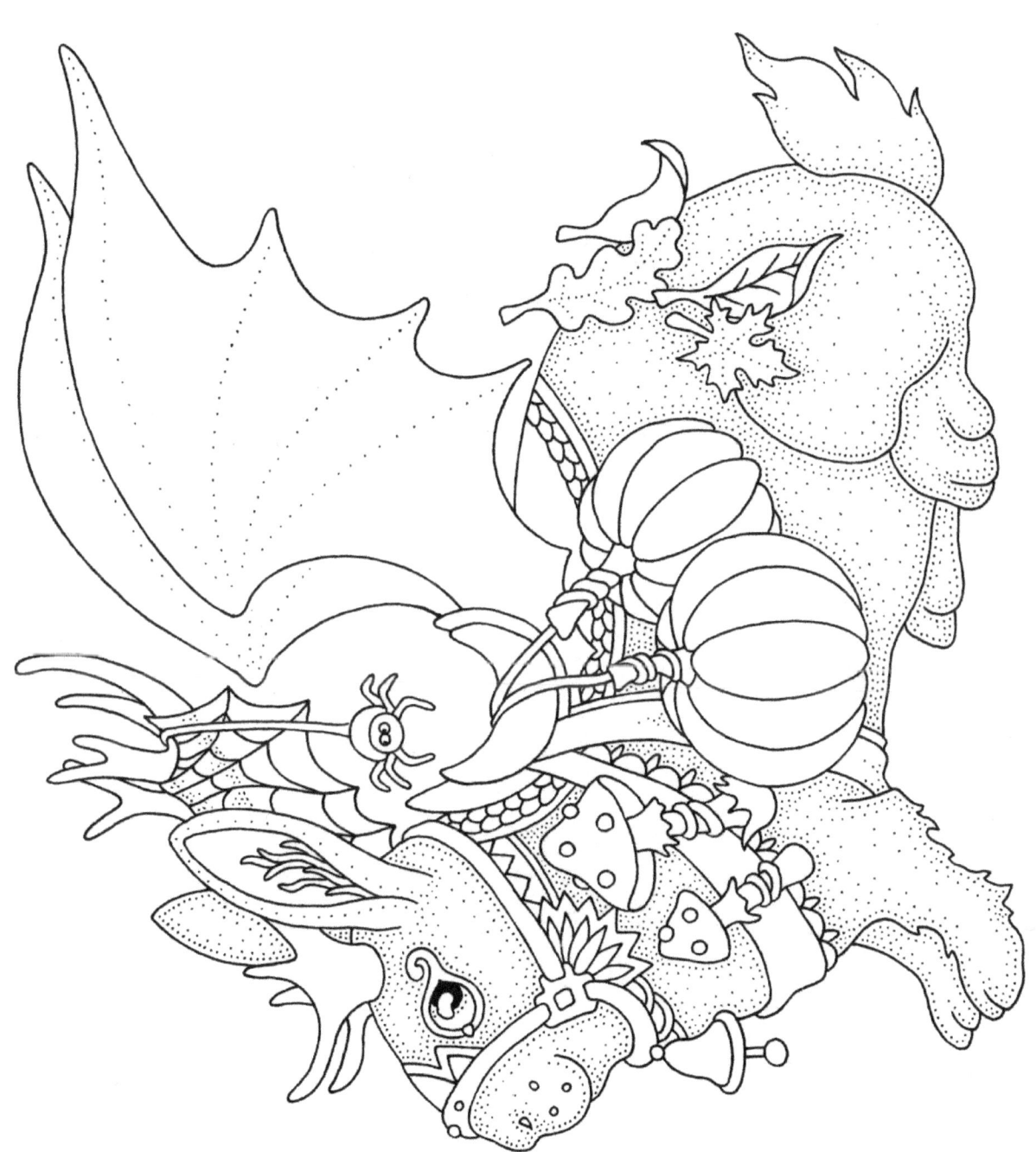

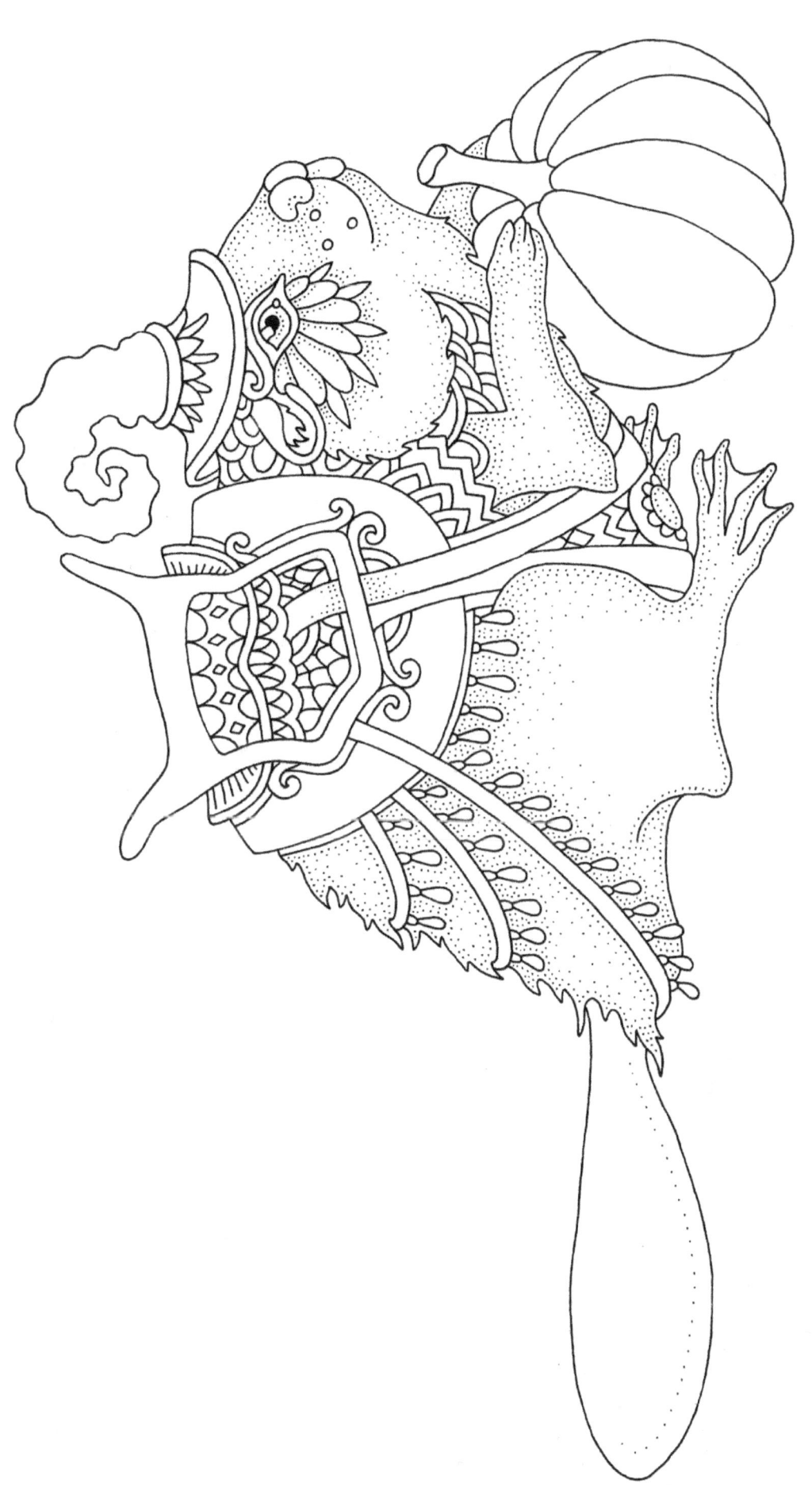

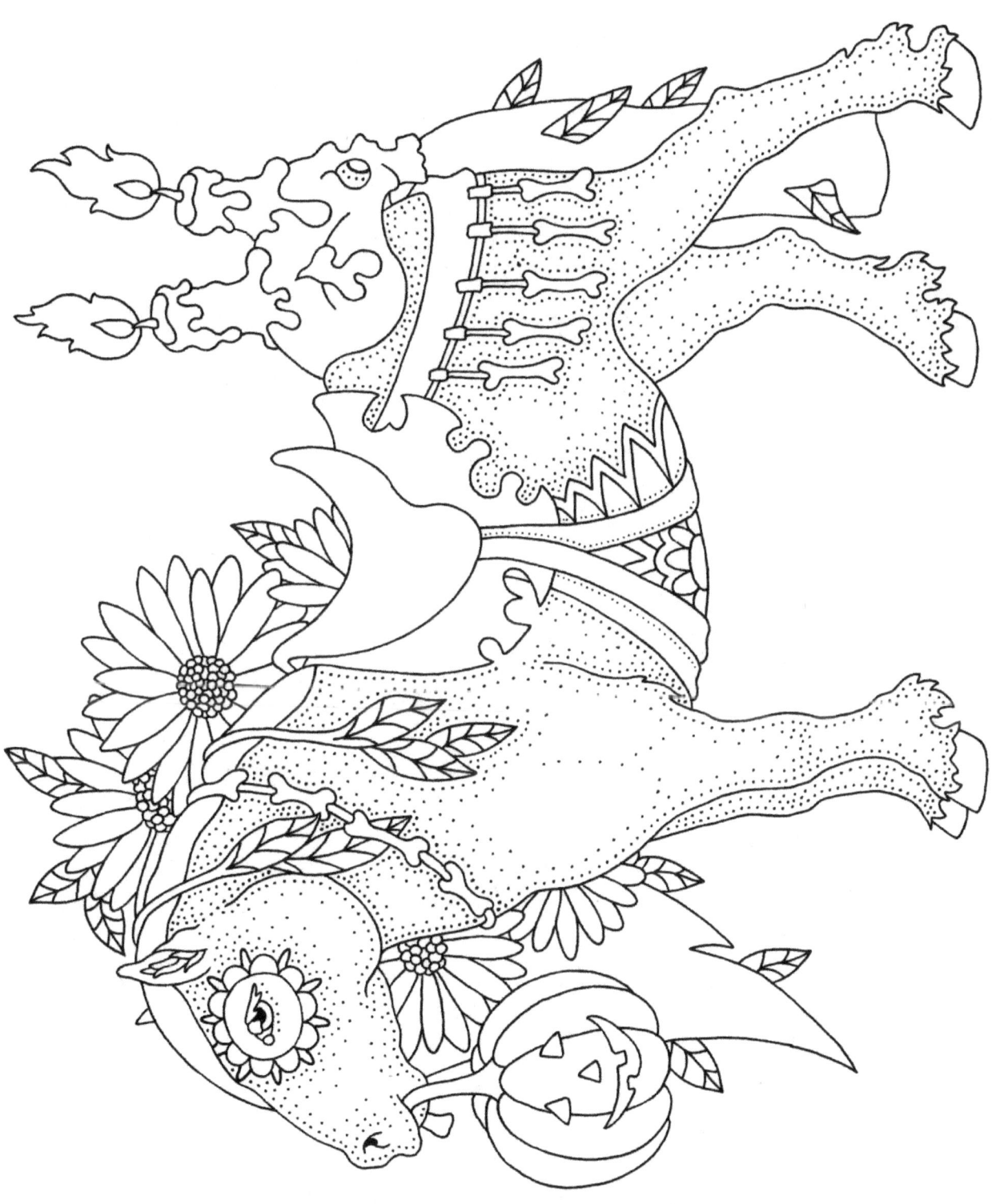

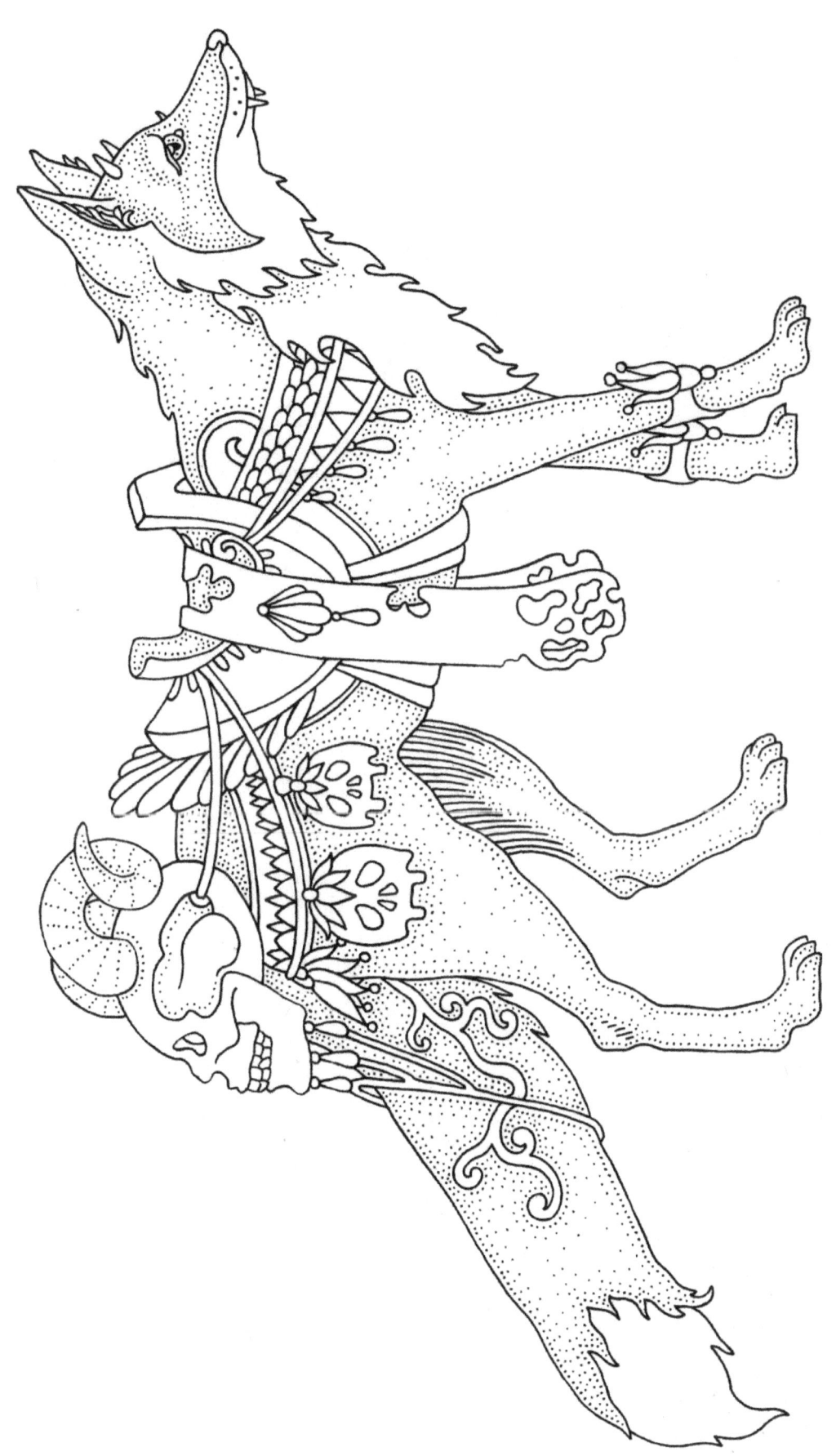

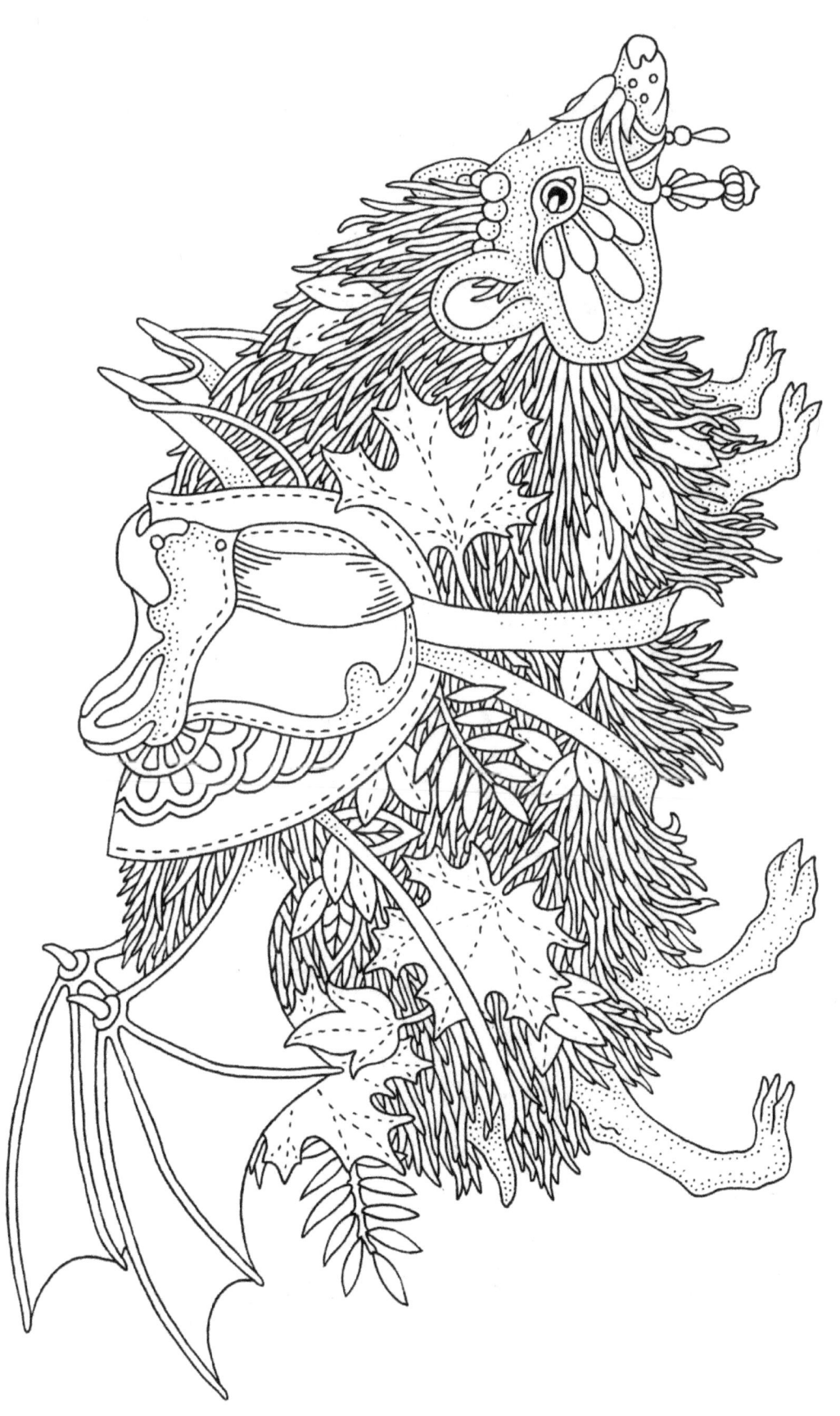

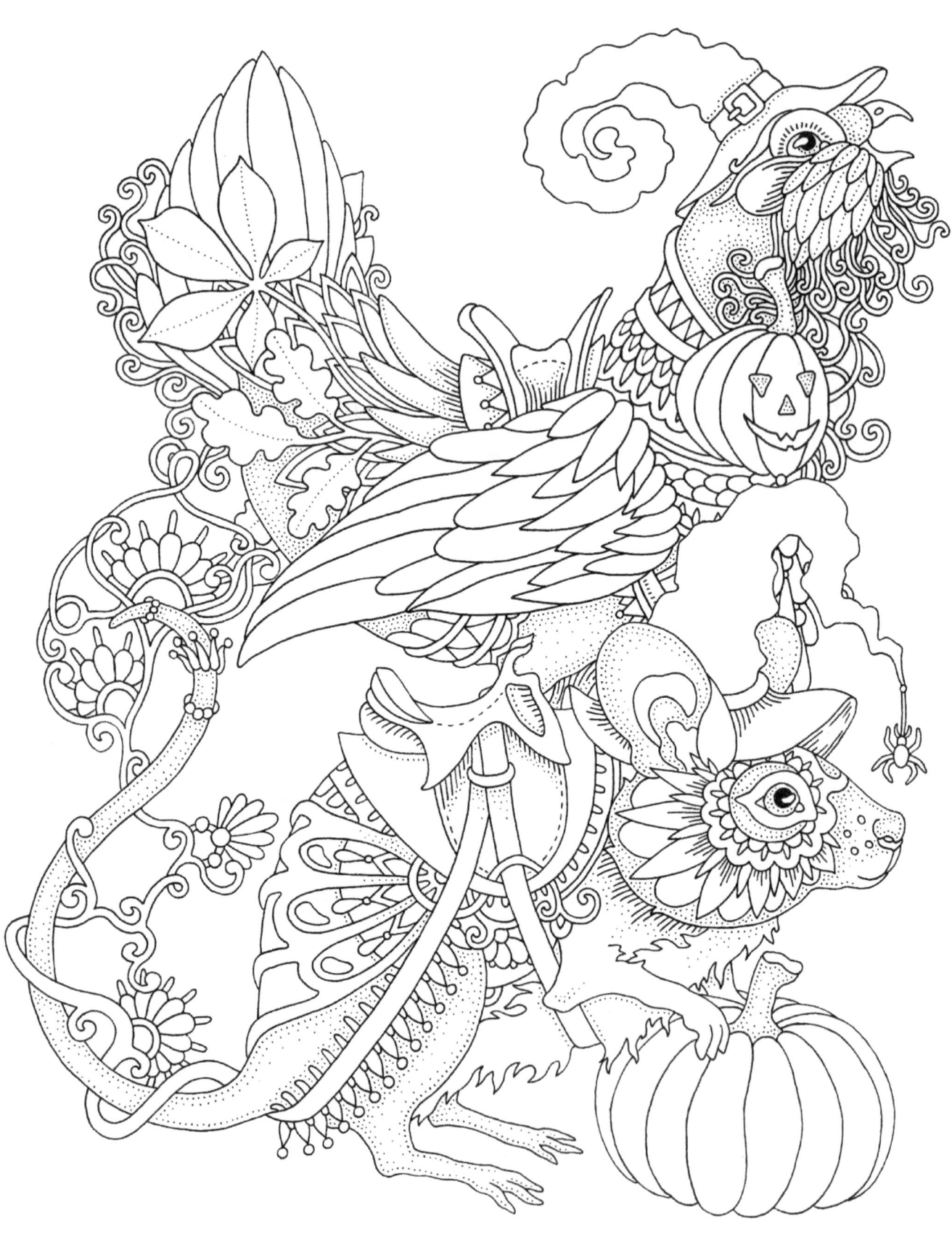

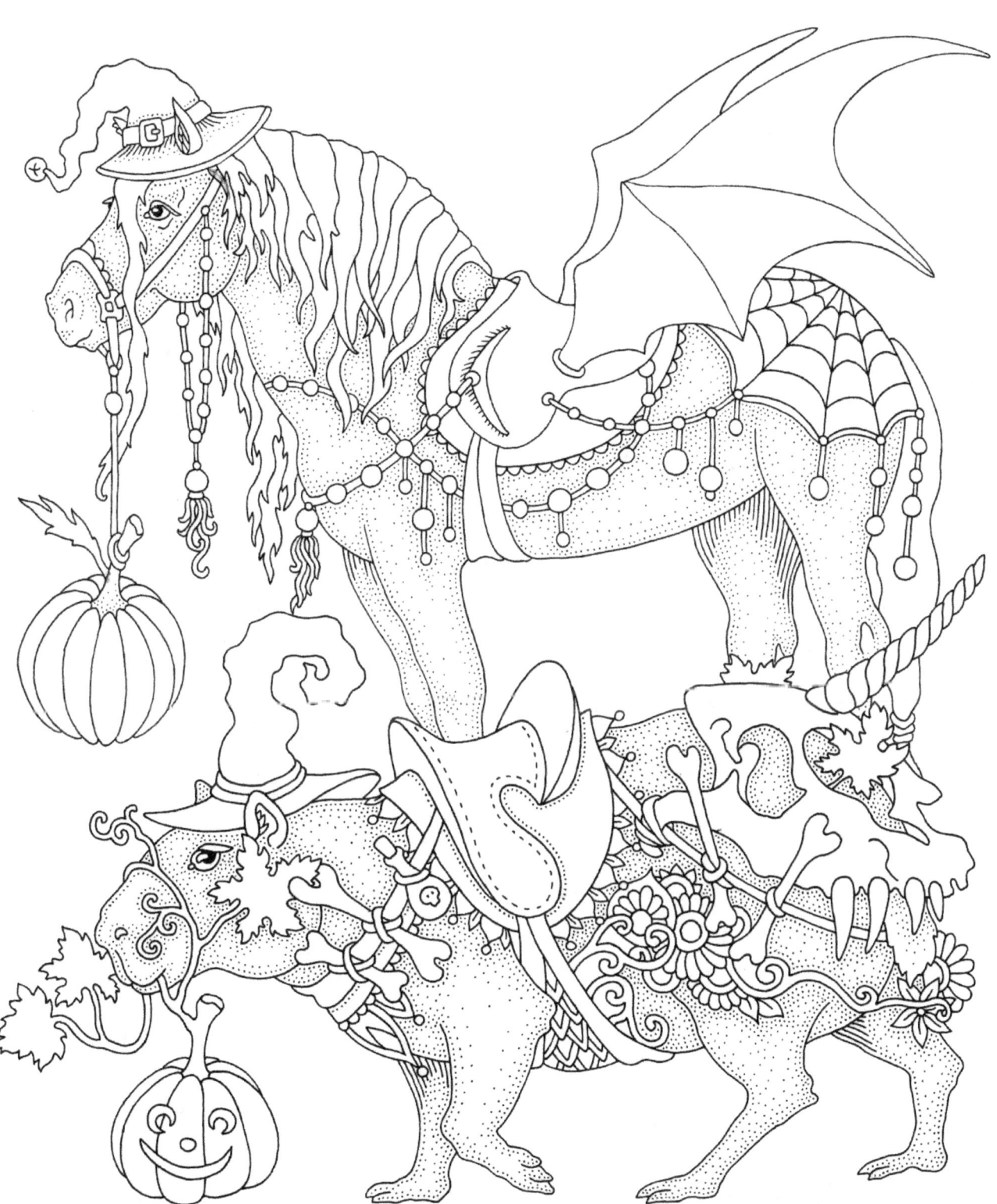